IARIA

ALLSENSORS 2017

The Second International Conference on Advances in Sensors, Actuators, Metering and Sensing

March 19 – 23, 2017

Nice, France

ALLSENSORS 2017 Editors

Sandrine Bernardini, Aix Marseille University, France
Paulo E. Cruvinel, Embrapa Instrumentation, Brazil

Printed from e-media with permission by:

Curran Associates, Inc.
57 Morehouse Lane
Red Hook, NY 12571

Some format issues inherent in the e-media version may also appear in this print version.

Printed by Curran Associates, Inc. (2017)

International Academy, Research, and Industry Association (IARIA)
412 Derby Way
Wilmington, DE 19810

Phone: (408) 893-6407
Fax: (408) 527-6351

petre@iaria.org

Additional copies of this publication are available from:

Curran Associates, Inc.
57 Morehouse Lane
Red Hook, NY 12571 USA
Phone: 845-758-0400
Fax: 845-758-2633
Email: curran@proceedings.com
Web: www.proceedings.com

Table of Contents

Design of a High-speed CMOS Image Sensor with an Intelligent Digital Correlated Double Sampling and a Symmetrical 3-Input Comparator 1
Minhyun Jin, Daehyuck Kim, and MIinkyu Song

Pet Food Industry: E-nose and E-tongue Technology for Quality Control 5
Federica Cheli, Martina Novacco, Valentino Bontempo, and Vittorio Dell'Orto

Design and Fabrication of Sensor Chip with Heater for Semiconductor Flip-Chip Package Application 8
Boo Taek Lim, Young-Su Kim, Nam Soo Park, and Boung Ju Lee

Using the Measurement-based Approach to Emulate the Behavior of a Sensor for Internal Hydraulic Pressure Drop Measurements of Sprayers in the Agricultural Industry 10
Rafael Magossi, Elmer Penaloza, Shankar Battachharya, Vilma Oliveira, and Paulo Cruvinel

Low-cost Gas Concentration Sensor System 16
Axel Kramer, Teresa Jorge, Mariya Porus, and Thomas Alfred Paul

Optical Detection of Lesions in the Depth of a Solid Breast Phantom 18
Anett Bailleu, Axel Hagen, Rene Freyer, and Dirk Grosenick

Effects of theWSN Deployment Environment on MaxMin and LQI-DCP Multihop Clustering Protocols 24
Cherif Diallo

Multi Objective Nodes Placement Approach in WSN based on Nature Inspired Optimisation Algorithms 30
Faten Hajjej, Ridha Ejbali, and Mourad Zaied

Hydrogen Peroxide Vapours Sensors Made From ZnO<La> and SnO2<Co> Films 36
Vladimir Aroutiounian, Valeri Arakelyan, Mikael Aleksanyan, Artak Sayunts, Gohar Shahnazaryan, Petr Kacer, Pavel Picha, Jiri Kovarik, Jakub Pekarek, and Berndt Joost

Comparaison between MOX Sensors for Low VOCs Concentrations with Interfering Gases 39
Frank James, Tomas Fiorido, Marc Bendahan, and Khalifa Aguir

Studies of Resistive-type Hydrogen-Sensitive Sensors Using Pd-Based Thin Films 41
Hao Lo, Chieh Lo, Jian-Hong Wu, and Wen-Shiung Lour

Study of Propylene Glycol and Dimethylformamide Vapors Sensors Based on MWCNTs/SnO2 Nanocomposites 44
Zaven Adamyan, Artak Sayunts, Vladimir Aroutiounian, Emma Khachaturyan, Arsen Adamyan, Martin Vrnata, Premysl Fitl, and Jan Vlcek

Ab Initio Investigation of CO Gas Sensing Mechanism on SnO2 Surfaces 50

Hayk Zakaryan and Vladimir Aroutiounian

Aluminum-doped Zinc Oxide Nanocrystals for NO2 Detection at Low Temperature 56
Sandrine Bernardini, Bruno Lawson, Olivier Margeat, Khalifa Aguir, Christine Videlot-Ackermann, and Jorg Ackermann

Area and Speed Efficient Layout Design of Shift Registers using Nanometer Technology 58
Rajesh Mehra, Priya Kaushal, and Ayushi Gagneja

ALLSENSORS 2017

Forward

The Second International Conference on Advances in Sensors, Actuators, Metering and Sensing (ALLSENSORS 2017), held in Nice, France, March 19 - 23, 2017, follows the inaugural event covering related topics on theory practice and applications of sensor devices, techniques, data acquisition and processing, and on wired and wireless sensors and sensor networks.

Sensor networks and sensor-based systems support many applications today above ground. Underwater operations and applications are quite limited by comparison. Most applications refer to remotely controlled submersibles and wide-area data collection systems at a coarse granularity. Other remote sensing domains and applications are using special sensing devices and services. Transducers and actuators complement the monitoring and control and constitute an area of interest related to sensors. They make use of specific sensor-based measurements and convey appropriate control actions.

ALLSENSORS 2017 was intended to serve as a forum for researchers from the academia and the industry, professionals, standard developers, policy makers, investors and practitioners to present their recent results, to exchange ideas, and to establish new partnerships and collaborations.

The accepted papers covered a large spectrum of topics on techniques and applications, best practices, awareness and experiences as well as future trends and needs (both in research and practice) related to all aspects of sensor-based applications and services.

We take here the opportunity to warmly thank all the members of the ALLSENSORS 2017 technical program committee as well as the numerous reviewers. The creation of such a broad and high quality conference program would not have been possible without their involvement. We also kindly thank all the authors that dedicated much of their time and efforts to contribute to the ALLSENSORS 2017. We truly believe that thanks to all these efforts, the final conference program consists of top quality contributions.

This event could also not have been a reality without the support of many individuals, organizations and sponsors. In addition, we also gratefully thank the members of the ALLSENSORS 2017 organizing committee for their help in handling the logistics and for their work that is making this professional meeting a success.

We hope the ALLSENSORS 2017 was a successful international forum for the exchange of ideas and results between academia and industry and to promote further progress on the topics of sensors.

We also hope that Nice provided a pleasant environment during the conference and everyone saved some time for exploring this beautiful city.

ALLSENSORS 2017 Chairs

ALLSENSORS Steering Committee

ALLSENSORS Industry/Research Advisory Committee

ALLSENSORS 2017

COMMITTEE

ALLSENSORS Steering Committee

Sergey Yurish, Excelera, S. L. | IFSA, Spain
Michael Niedermayer, Beuth University of Applied Sciences - Berlin, Germany
Jagannathan Sarangapani, Missouri University of Science and Technology, USA
Qingsong Xu, University of Macau, Macau, China
Càndid Reig, University of Valencia, Spain
Sandrine Bernardini, Aix Marseille University, France
Gholamreza Alirezaei, Institute for Theoretical Information Technology | RWTH Aachen University, Germany
Tamer Nadeem, Old Dominion University, USA

ALLSENSORS Industry/Research Advisory Committee

Paulo E. Cruvinel, Embrapa Instrumentation, Brazil
Yuriy S. Shmaliy, Universidad de Guanajuato, Mexico
Suzanne Lesecq, LIALP - Commissariat à l'énergie atomique et aux énergies alternatives MINATEC Campus, France
Xin Wang, Qualcomm, Inc., USA
Matteo Tonezzer, Italian National Research Council - Institute of Materials for Electronics and Magnetism (CNR - IMEM), Italy

ALLSENSORS 2017 Technical Program Committee

Amin Al-Habaibeh, Nottingham Trent University, UK
Wael Y. Alghamdi, University of New South Wales, Australia
Falah H. Ali, University of Sussex, UK
Gholamreza Alirezaei, Institute for Theoretical Information Technology | RWTH Aachen University, Germany
Anett Bailleu, Hochschule für Technik und Wirtschaft Berlin, Germany
Sandrine Bernardini, Aix Marseille University, France
Paula María Castro Castro, Universidade da Coruña, Spain
Omar Cheikhrouhou, Taif University, KSA
Nan-Fu Chiu, National Taiwan Normal University, Taiwan
Adriano Cola, CNR- IMM (National Council of Research - Institute of Microelectronics and Microsystems), Italy
Paulo E. Cruvinel, Embrapa Instrumentation, Brazil
Madhavrao K. Deore, Arts, Science and Commerce College, Ozar (Mig), India
Emiliano Descrovi, Politecnico di Torino, Italy
Javad Foroughi, University of Wollongong, Australia
Daniel Hill, The Institute for Molecular Science (ICMol) - Universitat de Valencia, Spain
Carmen Horrillo, ITEFI-CSIC, Madrid, Spain
Wei Min Huang, Nanyang Technological University, Singapore
Yanqiu Huang, University of Bremen, Germany
Md. Rajibul Islam, University of Malaya, Malaysia

Ahmed Abu Ismaiel, Municipality of Abasan Al-Kabira, Gaza, Palestine
Rajan Jha, Indian Institute of Technology Bhubaneswar, India
Anand Y. Joshi, G.H. Patel College of Engineering & Technology, Gujarat, India
Taeho Jung, Illinois Institute of Technology, USA
Grigoris Kaltsas, Technological Educational Institute (T.E.I) of Athens, Greece
Amarjeet Kaur, University of Delhi, India
Roman Kolcun, Imperial College London, UK
Boris Kovalerchuk, Central Washington University, USA
M. Bala Krishna, USICT, Guru Gobind Singh Indraprastha University, India
Seongsoo Lee, Soongsil University, Korea
Suzanne Lesecq, LIALP - Commissariat à l'énergie atomique et aux énergies alternatives MINATEC Campus, France
Jing-Sin Liu, Institute of Information Science | Academia Sinica, Taiwan
Yu-Lung Lo, National Cheng Kung University (NCKU), Taiwan
Vladimir Lukin, National Aerospace University, Kharkov, Ukraine
Bodh Raj Mehta, Indian Institute of Technology Delhi, India
Marek Miskowicz, AGH University of Science and Technology, Poland
Tamer Nadeem, Old Dominion University, USA
Michael Niedermayer, Beuth University of Applied Sciences - Berlin, Germany
Michael O'Grady, University College Dublin, Ireland
Min-Chun Pan, National Central University (NCU), Taiwan
Devidas Ramrao Patil, Rani Laxmibai Mahavidyalaya Parola, Jalgaon, India
Luigi Patrono, University of Salento, Italy
Rajinikumar Ramalingam, Karlsruhe Institute for Technology, Germany
Reza Rashidi, State University of New York - Alfred State College, USA
Càndid Reig, University of Valencia, Spain
Christos Riziotis, National Hellenic Research Foundation, Greece
Bahram Djafari Rouhani, Université de Lille 1 Sciences et Technologies, France
Jagannathan (Jag) Sarangapani, Missouri University of Science and Technology, USA
Chayan Sarkar, SICS Swedish ICT AB, Sweden
Leonello Servoli, Istituto Nazionale di Fisica Nucleare, Perugia, Italy
Yuriy S. Shmaliy, Universidad de Guanajuato, Mexico
Marius Silaghi, Florida Institute of Technology, USA
Cristian Stanciu, University Politehnica of Bucharest, Romania
Mu-Chun Su, National Central University, Taiwan
Ryszard Tadeusiewicz, AGH University of Science and Technology, Krakow, Poland
Pedro Renato Tavares Pinho, ISEL / Instituto de Telecomunicações, Portugal
Matteo Tonezzer, Italian National Research Council - Institute of Materials for Electronics and Magnetism (CNR - IMEM), Italy
Federico Tramarin, National Research Council of Italy - CNR-IEIIT, Padova, Italy
Pere Tuset-Peiró, Universitat Oberta de Catalunya, Spain
Xin Wang, Qualcomm Inc, USA
Magnus Willander, Linköping University, Sweden
Qingsong Xu, University of Macau, China
Zhengwei Yang, Zhengwei Yang, United States Department of Agriculture / George Mason University, USA
Sergey Yurish, Excelera, S. L. | IFSA, Spain

Pengfei Zhang, Nanyang Technological University, Singapore
Jianhua Zhou, Sun Yat-Sen University, China

Copyright Information

Design of a High-speed CMOS Image Sensor with an Intelligent Digital Correlated Double Sampling and a Symmetrical 3-Input Comparator

Minhyun Jin, Daehyuck Kim, and Minkyu Song
Department of Semiconductor Science, Dongguk University,
3-26, Phil-dong, Choong-ku, Seoul, Korea
E-mail : mhjin91@naver.com, dh7423@dongguk.edu, mksong@dongguk.edu

Abstract— **In order to improve the frame rate of a CMOS image sensor (CIS), a novel technique of correlated double sampling (CDS) and a symmetrical 3-input comparator are discussed. In the conventional digital CDS, a subtraction algorithm between the reset digital code and the pixel digital code has been normally adopted. Thus, it needs two ramps and takes a much more operating time, compared to that of analog CDS. In this paper, an intelligent digital CDS is proposed drastically to reduce the operating time. Further, a symmetrical 3-input comparator to implement the intelligent digital CDS is also described. A high speed CIS with the proposed CDS and a symmetrical 3-input comparator has been fabricated with Samsung 0.13um CIS technology. A high frame rate of 240fps is achieved at the VGA resolution of 640x480 with 39mW power consumption.**

Keywords—CMOS image sensor(CIS); one-ramp digital correlated double sampling; symmetrical 3-input comparator; subtraction algorithm.

I. INTRODUCTION

CMOS Image Sensors (CIS) are now widely used in many kinds of areas including digital cameras, camcorders, CCTV cameras, medical equipment, etc. In order to improve the image quality of CIS, research has focused on developing methods to reduce noise. In CIS, Fixed Pattern Noise (FPN) is a major factor causing the degradation of image quality. FPN is normally generated from the device mismatching errors of pixel circuits, such as threshold voltage variations of source follower, fluctuations of MOS transistor size, etc. To remove the errors, a few techniques of analog Correlated Double Sampling (CDS) have been reported [1][2]. However, it requires a large size of capacitor to enhance the accuracy. Further, it is difficult to have a high resolution image beyond 8-bit. Therefore, many CISs with a single-slope ADC use a digital CDS to reduce FPN [3]-[10]. In the digital CDS, FPN is normally eliminated by comparing the reset signal and the pixel signal through the two ramp signals. Generally, the length of the reset ramp signal is at least about a quarter of the pixel ramp signal. In other words, the A/D conversion time of digital CDS is much longer than that of analog CDS only. Even though the digital CDS has a high quality image, the operating speed is much lower than that of analog CDS. In this paper, to improve the speed of CIS, a single ramp signal is used. The contents of the papers are as follows. In Section II, the conventional CDS and a new CDS are discussed. The implementation of CIS and experimental results are described in Section III. Finally, the conclusions are summarized in Section IV.

II. CORRELATED DOUBLE SAMPLING (CDS)

In order to understand the main idea of this paper, the principle of CDS is essential. After a conventional CDS is described, the proposed CDS technique will be discussed.

A. Conventional Two-ramps Digital CDS

Fig. 1 shows a conventional CIS with a single-slope ADC (SS-ADC). Fig. 1(a) shows the block diagram of a CIS with a column parallel ADC. Since it consists of many pixels, the pixel FPN can occur due to device mismatching errors. The pixel FPN conveys each output from the same light to the ADC in the form of another voltage. Moreover, the ADC in each column can also generate imbalance features, column FPN. Therefore, both the pixel FPN and the column FPN must be reduced and properly calibrated. In order to reduce the FPN, an SS-ADC with an analog CDS shown in Fig. 1(b) is widely used. The difference between the pixel signal voltage and the reset voltage is transferred into ADC [3]-[6].

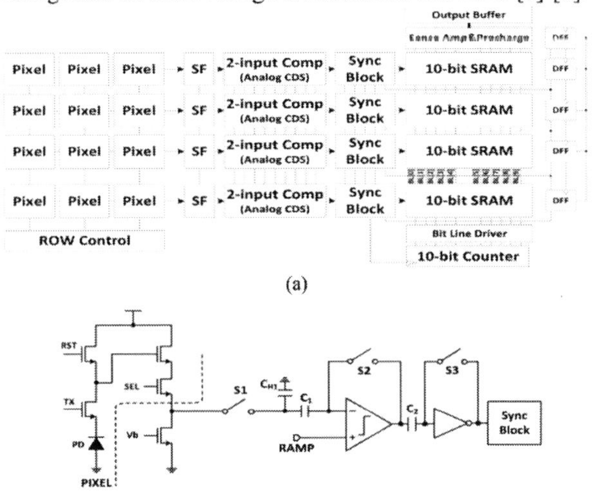

Figure 1. Principle of a Conventional CMOS Image Sensor (CIS)
(a) Block Diagram (b) Circuit Diagram for a CDS

The analog CDS requires a large size of the capacitor to enhance the accuracy. Thus, a digital CDS is generally used with an analog CDS in order to reduce FPN. Fig. 2 shows the timing diagram of the conventional SS-ADC with a digital CDS. It compares the reset signal with the first ramp and the pixel signal with the second ramp. When comparing the reset signal, the counter executes a down count mode. When comparing pixel signal, the counter operates in the up count mode. In this case, the digital CDS can remove the FPN that cannot be removed with the analog CDS. However, the conversion time of digital CDS is increased because an additional ramp is needed at the SS-ADC, compared to that of analog CDS. Generally, the operation time to compare the reset signal with the ramp is about a quarter of the time to compare the pixel signal with the ramp. Therefore, the A/D conversion time of digital CDS is much longer than that of analog CDS only.

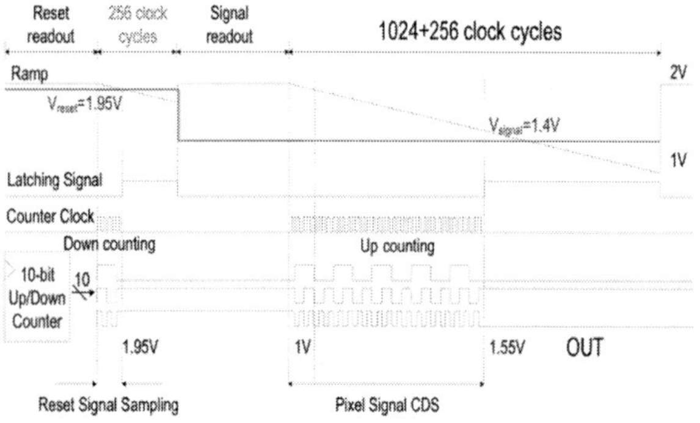

Figure 2. Timing Diagram of a Conventional Two-ramps Digital CDS

B. *Intelligent CDS*

Fig. 3 shows the principle of a SS-ADC with the proposed intelligent digital CDS. Fig. 3(a) shows the circuit diagram of a SS-ADC with the intelligent CDS. Instead of a conventional comparator, a symmetrical 3-input comparator performs an A/D conversion. In order to separate the voltage coming from the reset signal and the pixel signal, a holding capacitor and a DC blocking capacitor are used at each node, respectively. Fig. 3(b) shows the circuit diagram of 3-input comparator, and Fig. 3(c) shows the timing diagram of a SS-ADC. Since the reset signal and the pixel signal are stored separately through the operation of the intelligent CDS, only one ramp signal is enough to obtain a digital code even in a digital CDS. The procedure of Fig. 3(c) is as follows. In the region of A, the reset signal is stored at C_{H1} when S1 and S3 are ON, then the pixel signal is stored at C_{H2} when S2 and S4 are ON. Further, in Fig. 3(b), when S6 and S8 are ON, S7 and S9 are OFF, the 3-input comparator is now ready to start.

In the region of B, all the switches of Fig. 3(a), S1,S2,S3, and S4 are OFF. Then, the ramp is now starting down when S6 and S9 are ON, S7 and S8 are OFF in Fig. 3(b). Thus, the right side of 3-input comparator is at the state of equilibrium, and the left side of 3-input comparator amplifies the voltage difference between the ramp and the reset signal. The output voltage of 3-input comparator is easily obtained from the simple equation of a differential amplifier as follows.

$$V_{out} = G_m \ R_{out} \ \{(V_{RAMP} - V_{rst}) + (V_{sig} - V_{sig})\} \qquad (1)$$

where G_m is the input transconductance of 3-input comparator, R_{out} is the output impedance, respectively. At the end of region B, when the ramp signal and the reset signal are the same, the sync block becomes HIGH.

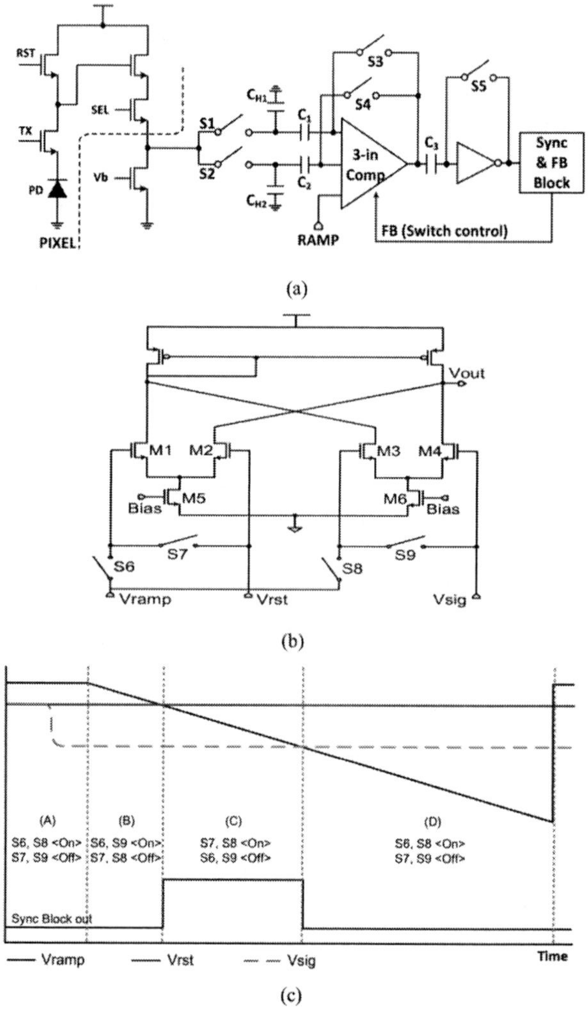

Figure 3. Principle of the Proposed CDS
(a) Circuit Diagram for an Intelligent one-ramp CDS
(b) Circuit Diagram for a Symmetrical 3-input Comparator
(c) Timing Diagram for the Switch Operation Procedure

In the region of C, the counter is starting to count, when S7 and S8 are ON, S6 and S9 are OFF, in Fig. 3(b). Thus, the left side of 3-input comparator is at the state of equilibrium, and the right side of 3-input comparator amplifies the voltage difference between the ramp and the pixel signal. At this time, the output voltage of 3-input comparator is also easily obtained as follows.

$$V_{out} = G_m \; R_{out} \; \{(V_{rst} - V_{rst}) + (V_{RAMP} - V_{sig})\} \qquad (2)$$

At the end of region C, when the ramp signal and the pixel signal are the same, the sync block becomes LOW and the counter stops. Therefore, the digital code which corresponds to the difference of reset signal and pixel signal can be calculated. The operating time of the intelligent CDS technique can be reduced drastically compared to that of a conventional CDS, because only one ramp is used. In the region of D, all the functions of 3-input comparator stop and it returns to the initial state, when S6 and S8 are ON, S7 and S9 are OFF. Thus, the 3-input comparator is like a symmetrical amplifier.

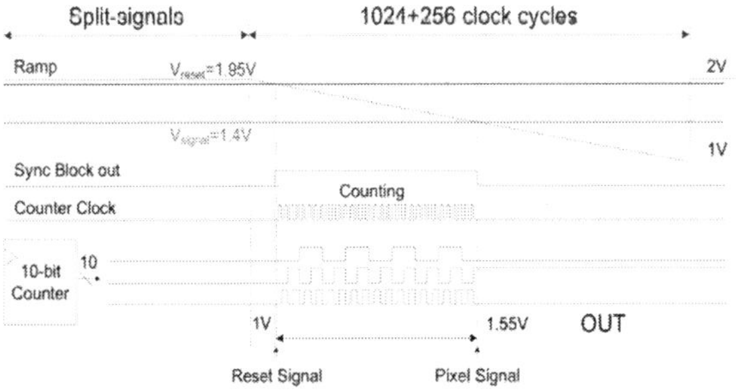

Figure 4. Timing Diagram of the Proposed Intelligent One-ramp CDS

Fig. 4 shows the timing diagram of a SS-ADC with the proposed intelligent digital CDS. Compared to those of Fig. 2, it does not need the section that compares the reset signal with the ramp. In case of 10-bit SS-ADC, at least, the time of 256 cycles is saved. Therefore, the operating time of the proposed technique is much faster than that of the conventional one.

III. Experimental Results

Fig. 5 shows the block diagram of a CIS with a 10-bit SS-ADC and the intelligent digital CDS. The CIS is based on a column-parallel ADC structure with a VGA resolution of 640x480, and each pixel uses a 4-TR APS with a size of 5.6 µm x 5.6 µm. As mentioned above, the CIS uses the intelligent digital CDS, which compares the reset signal and the pixel signal with only one ramp signal. Thereby, this new method facilitates the digital block with a simple counter. Because of a simple counter, the chip area of digital block is drastically reduced, compared to that of the conventional one.

Table I shows the comparison of chip size per one column. With 0.13µm Samsung CIS technology, the total layout size of the proposed one per one column is 470 µm, while that of a conventional one is 450 µm. Thus, the total chip area of the proposed CIS is not so much bigger than that of the conventional one, even though the intelligent digital CDS technique uses the large size of capacitors and differential mode at the analog block.

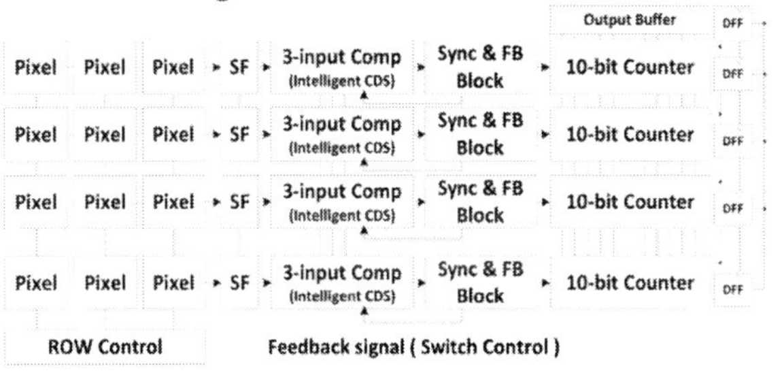

Figure 5. Block Diagram of the CIS with an Intelligent CDS

TABLE I. CHIP SIZE COMPARISON PER ONE COLUMN

	Counter	Capacitor	total
Conventional one (10-bit)	330 µm (up-down)	120 µm (1.5pF)	450 µm
This work (10-bit)	230 µm (normal)	240 µm (3pF)	470 µm
Column pitch = 11.2 µm C1, C2 = 500fF CH1, CH2 = 1pF Unit capacitor = 50fF (L=7 µm, W=4 µm)			

Fig. 6(a) shows the chip microphotograph of the CIS fabricated with Samsung 0.13 µm 1P4M CIS technology. The chip size is 6 mm x 6 mm, and the pixel array conforms to the VGA resolution (640x480). Fig. 6(b) shows the configuration of the measurement system which is comprised of a board that contains the Xilinx-XEM 3050 FPGA and a test board of the prototype CIS chip with a chip-on-board (COB). The prototype of CIS chip shown in Fig. 6(a) is controlled by the control signals through an external FPGA. Using such a configuration allows us to establish various test environments for the image sensor, to verify the performance of the CIS and to check the results of various features. The FPGA plays a role in generating the control signal for the measurements, receiving the output data from the image sensor, and delivering the results to the PC through the USB interface. The transmitted data are handled in the PC, where the real image is processed.

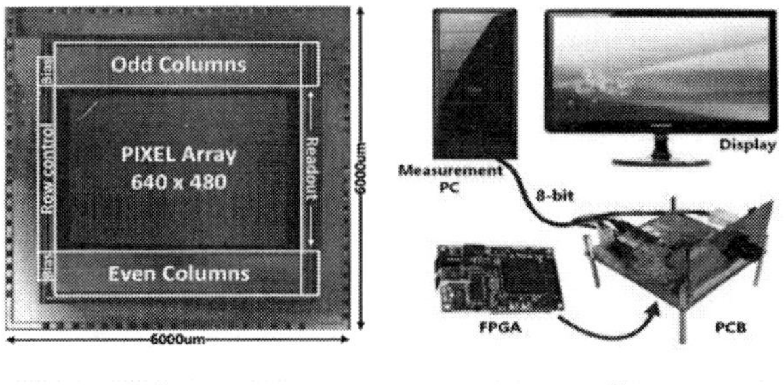

(a) (b)

Figure 6. Chip Photo and Measurement (a)Chip Microphotograph of the CIS with Samsung 0.13µm CIS (b) Configuration of the Measurement Systems

Figure 7. Measured VGA Sample Image

Fig. 7 shows the VGA sample image with the condition of 10-bit resolution. The method achieves frame rates of 240 fps at a main clock speed of 100MHz. The image shows high quality.

IV. CONCLUSION

A high speed CMOS image sensor with an intelligent digital CDS technique was discussed. In order to raise the operating speed of the conventional CIS, we described a new symmetrical 3-input comparator and an intelligent digital CDS that compares the reset signal and the pixel signal using only one ramp. With the technique, the operating speed of the proposed CIS was much faster than that of the conventional one, because only one ramp was adopted. The prototype chip has been fabricated with the Samsung 0.13 μm 1P4M CIS technology. The resolution of the CMOS image sensor was the VGA specifications of 640x480, and the pixel size was 5.6 μm with the 4-TR APS. The conversion time of the designed 10-bit SS-ADC using the intelligent digital CDS satisfied the 16-μs at a main clock speed of 100MHz. The frame rate of the CIS was of 240 fps at the main clock speed of 100MSPS. Table II shows the comparison results of the proposed CDS with the previously published works. The proposed CIS has the advantage of high speed frame rate, compared to other ones at the same condition.

TABLE II PERFORMANCE COMPARISON

Reference	[7]	[8]	[9]	[10]	This work
Technology	0.13um	0.18um	0.13um	0.18um	0.13um
CDS	Analog	Digital	Digital	Analog	Digital
ADC Type	Sigma-delta	Single-slope	Single-slope	TS Cyclic	Single-slope
ADC Bit	11-bit	10&12-bit,	12&14-bit	12-bit	10-bit
Pixel Array	1600x1300	1920 x 1440	8192 x 2160	76804320	640 x 480
Frame Rate	120	180 (10-bit)	120 (12-bit)	120	240
Power [mW]	44.1	580	3000	2500	39.2

In the future, we have a plan to raise the pixel array up to UHD resolution (3840 x 2160), the frame rate up to 360, and the ADC resolution up to 14-bit. Further, a two-step single-slope ADC with the proposed CDS technique will also be studied.

ACKNOWLEDGMENT

This research was supported by Basic Science Research Program through the National Research Foundation of Korea(NRF) funded by the Ministry of Education, Science and Technology(2015R1A1A2001455).

REFERENCES

[1] T. Sugiki, S. Ohsawa, H. Miura, M. Sasaki, N. Nakamura, I. Inoue, M. Hoshino, Y. Tomizawa, and T. Arakawa, "A 60 mW 10 b CMOS image sensor with column-to-column FPN reduction," in Proc. IEEE ISSCC Dig. Tech. Papers, pp. 108-109, Feb. 2000.

[2] S. Lim, J. Cheon, S. Ham, and G. Han, "A new correlated double sampling and single slope ADC circuit for CMOS image sensors," in Proc. Int. SoC Des. Conf., pp. 129–131, Oct. 2004

[3] F. Snoeij, A. Theuwissen, K. Makinwa, and J. Huijsing, "Multiple-ramp column-parallel ADC architectures for CMOS image sensors," IEEE J. Solid-State Circuits, vol. 42, no. 12, ,pp. 2968–2967, Dec. 2007.

[4] S. Yoshihara, M. Kikuchi, Y. Ito, Y. Inada, S. Kuramochi, H. Wakabayashi, M. Okano, K. Koseki, H. Kuriyama, J. Inutsuka, A. Tajima, T. Nakajima, Y. Kudoh, F. Koga, Y. Kasagi, S. Watanabe, and T. Nomoto, "A 1/1.8-inch 6.4Mpixel 60 frames/s CMOS image sensor with seamless mode change," IEEE J. Solid-State Circuits, vol. 41, no. 12, pp. 2998–3006, Dec. 2006.

[5] A. I. Krymski, N. E. Bock, N. Tu, D. V. Blerkom, and E. R. Fossum, "A high-speed, 240-frames/s, 4.1-Mpixel CMOS sensor" IEEE Trans. Electron Devices, vol. 50, no. 1, pp. 130–135, Jan. 2003.

[6] W. Yang, O. B. Kwon, J. I. Lee, G. T. Hwang, and S. J. Lee, "An integrated 800×600 CMOS imaging system," ISSCC Dig. Tech. Papers, pp. 304-305, Feb. 1999.

[7] Y. Chae, J. Cheon, S. Lim, M. Kwon, K. Yoo, W. Jung, D. H. Lee, S. Ham, and G. Han, "A 2.1 Mpixels, 120 frame/s CMOS image sensor with column-parallel ΔΣ ADC architecture," IEEE J. Solid-State Circuits, vol. 46, no. 1, pp. 236-247, Jan. 2011.

[8] Y. Nita, Y. Muramatsu, K. Amano, T. Toyama, J. Yamamoto, K. Mishina, A. Suzuki, T. Taura, A. Kato, and M. Kikuchi, "High-Speed Digital Double Sampling with Analog CDS on Column Parallel ADC Architecture for Low-Noise Active Pixel Sensor" IEEE ISSCC Dig. Tech. Papers, pp. 2024-2031, Feb., 2006.

[9] T. Toyama, K. Mishina, H. Tsuchiya, T. Ichikawa, H. Iwaki, Y. Gendai, H. Murakami, K. Takamiya, H. Shiroshita, Y. Muramatsu, and T. Furusawa, "A 17.7Mpixel 120fps CMOS Image Sensor with 34.8Gb/s Readout," IEEE ISSCC Dig. Tech. Papers, pp. 420–422, Feb. 2011.

[10] T. Watabe, K. Kitamura, T. Sawamoto, T. Kosugi, T. Akahori, T. Iida, K. Isobe, T. Watanabe, H. Shimamoto, H. Ohtake, S. Aoyama, S. Kawahito, and N. Egami, "A 33Mpixel 120 fps CMOS Image Sensor for UDTV Application with Two-stage Column-Parallel Cyclic ADCs," IEEE ISSCC Dig. Tech. Papers, pp. 388-393, Feb. 2012.

Pet Food Industry: E-nose and E-tongue Technology for Quality Control

Federica Cheli, Martina Novacco, Valentino Bontempo, Vittorio Dell'Orto
Department of Health, Animal Science and Food Safety
Università degli Studi di Milano, Milano, Italy
e-mail: federica.cheli@unimi.it, martina.novacco@unimi.it, valentino.bontempo@unimi.it, vittorio.dellorto@unimi.it

Abstract — **The objective of this idea is to set up an electronic nose (e-nose) and tongue (e-tongue) as rapid quality control and research & development tools for the pet food industry. The final goal is to integrate e-nose and e-tongue with other sensing and imaging devices to 1) ensure high pet food standards in terms of nutritional properties, palatability and acceptability; 2) set up an instrumental protocol with good correlation to animal sensory properties in order to replace animal preference test, chemical and texture analysis.**

Keywords-pet food; palatability; electronic nose; electronic tongue.

I. INTRODUCTION

The pet food industry offers a wide range of products to satisfy pet's and owner's requirements. In pet food production, the development of new products must take into account both nutritional and palatability aspects. Pet food palatability is related to the pet food sensory properties, such as aroma, flavour, texture shape, and particle size [1]. Pet food formulation is one of the factors affecting its aromatic profile that is strictly associated with palatability and acceptability. Sensorial analysis of pet foods may be conducted by using several hedonic and analytical methods (Fig. 1) [2].

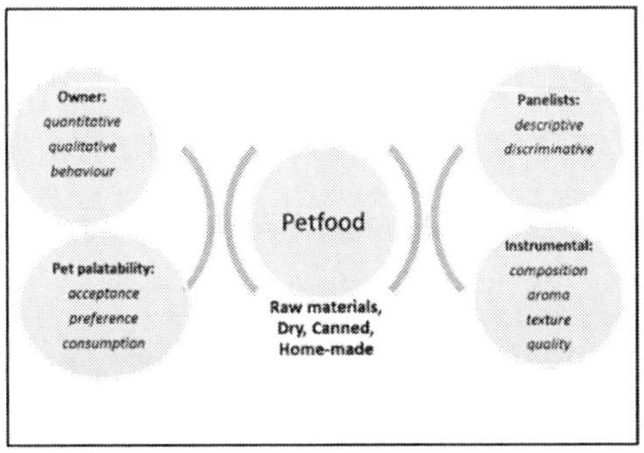

Figure 1. Pet food sensory analysis research methods.

Although taste and olfactory perceptions are not completely similar, dogs and cats use both taste and smell in food detection and selection [1][3]. Besides ingredient composition, pet food palatability may be affected by the use of palatability enhancers and food processing. Microbial growth, oxidation, and the presence of undesirable compounds and contaminants represent risk factors responsible of changes in aroma, flavours, and loss of palatability [4]. At the industry level, adoption of a rapid, low-cost, high-throughput and on-line analytical approach is needed at all stages of pet food production and processing in order to guarantee and standardize the quality of the production.

The objective of this idea is to set up an integrated e-nose and e-tongue technology as a rapid quality control and research & development tool for the pet food industry. To develop the idea, a step by step procedure must be designed: knowledge of e-nose and e-tongue characteristics and applications in the pet food industry, proper selection of an appropriate e-nose and e-tongue system for the specific application, and analysis of the pet food industry requirements.

II. THE ELECTRONIC NOSE AND ELECTRONIC TONGUE

The electronic nose (e-nose) is an instrument which comprises an array of electronic chemical sensors with partial specificity and an appropriate pattern recognition system, capable of recognizing simple or complex volatile organic compounds' (VOCs) patterns associated to a product odour. Researches have correlated VOCs to the sensory properties of a product; therefore, VOCs' profiles can be used for sensory characterisation and palatability evaluation of pet food [4]. The electronic tongue (e-tongue) has been developed in the last decade to evaluate the taste of liquid media. The common principle of the different e-tongue technologies is the application of an array of non-specific chemical sensors with high cross-sensitivity. To analyse results, similar pattern recognition techniques are needed for both the e-nose and e-tongue.

In literature, the applications of the e-nose and e-tongue in pet food analysis are very scarce. This could be attributed to the need to tune either the hardware and/or software to a specific application, or because data are kept confidentially by the product developers. E-nose associated or not with e-tongue has been used in studies for the standardization of a product development process, and in the quality control of the finished product [5]-[9]. In a study carried out in our department on commercial dry complete and dietetic dog and cat pet food, the e-nose was able to discriminate samples, although not completely, according to the species (dog *vs* cat), to the pet food formula (complete and balanced *vs* dietetic). Interestingly, e-nose was able to discriminate complete pet food for puppies or adult dogs (Fig. 2) [9].

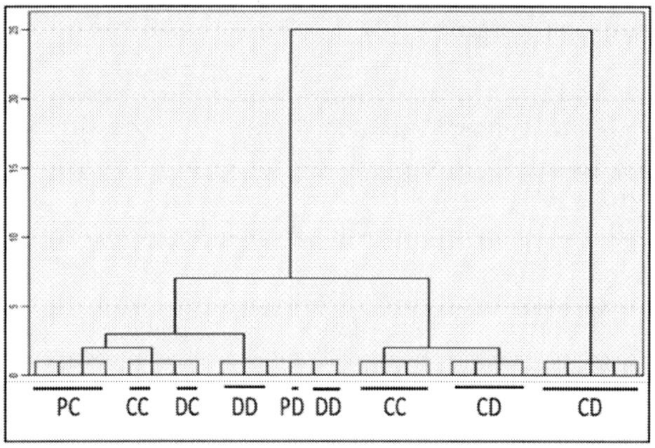

Figure 2. E-nose for dry pet food analysis (PC: puppy complete; DD: dog complete; CC: cat complete; PD: puppy dietetic; DD: dog dietetic CD: cat dietetic) (adapted from [9]).

In a study on commercial canned dog and cat pet food, similar results have been reported, with no complete discrimination obtained with e-nose analysis. A combination of e-nose and e-tongue determined a better discrimination between samples [7].

Although inconsistent results have been reported, e-nose and e-tongue may represent rapid and sensitive instrumental techniques for pet food evaluation. However, to represent an effective tool for a rapid quality control and research & development in the pet food industry, the analytical platform still needs several improvements, such as the definition of the best sensors' array, the development of data fusion analysis systems, and a better understanding of the industrial needs. The final aim of this idea is to develop an analytical sensory platform able to ensure high pet food standards in terms of nutritional properties, palatability and acceptability. The development of an instrumental protocol with good correlation to animal sensory properties could replace animal preference test, and chemical and texture analysis.

III. E-NOSE AND E-TONGUE IN AN INTEGRATED SYSTEM FOR PET FOOD EVALUATION

Domestic dogs and cats have different nutritional requirements and feeding behaviours, are sensitive to numerous palatability drivers, and differ in the food characteristics that they find desirable. Cats are strongly affected by the aroma of a food, and carefully smell a new food before tasting it. Dogs often prefer foods that are high in fat and include protein from animal sources. For both dogs and cats, the texture, size, and shape of food pieces are important aspects; scientists who study palatability refer to this as "mouth feel". Therefore, e-nose and e-tongue should be integrated in an instrumental platform to develop the full potential of an electronic sense analysis of pet food. Multi-sensor data fusion is an available technology capable of combining information from several sources in order to form a unified picture that can be used as a "finger print" of a product. A practical and general data fusion system model capable of handling data from various applications must be established on the basis of feature extraction. The final goal is to create a high-level fusion, namely decision-making fusion, able to analyse the features from each analytical system first, and then to associate these features to produce a fused result.

A. Set the e-nose and e-tongue for the specific application

A proper selection of an appropriate e-nose and e-tongue system for a particular application must involve an evaluation on a case-by-case basis. E-nose and e-tongue selection for a particular application must necessarily include: the assessment of the selectivity and the sensitivity range of individual sensor arrays for a particular target VOCs (i.e., related to the target organoleptic properties of the products), the number of unnecessary (redundancy) sensors with similar sensitivities, as well as sensor accuracy, reproducibility, response speed, recovery rate, robustness, and overall performance. Most of these steps are common points in a validation procedure. New ways to improve e-nose and e-tongue performance, through the use of better or more target-specific sensors, pattern-recognition algorithms, and data analysis methods will significantly amplify the range of applications of e-noses and e-tongue in the pet food industry.

B. An eye on the pet food industry requirements

According to The European Pet Food Industry Federation (FEDIAF), quality and safety, nutritional balance and palatability, variety and value for money, pet owner demands, and convenience are the important elements for pets and their owners. Feed material selection, processing, production techniques for canned or dry products, and final product quality and palatability control represent the critical processing points, which need and may take advantage from a real-time monitoring by the use of e-nose and/or e-tongue.

TABLE I. PET FOOD INDUSTRY: E-NOSE AND E-TONGUE FOR RESEARCH & DEVELOPMENT.

Main topics	Application areas
Palatants	flavour profile of new palatants for pets and identifications of key aromas and taste attributes
Palatability	Replace animal preference test, chemical and texture analysis
Brand	Characterisation of a quality brand

Besides quality control, e-nose and e-tongue may be used for research & development purposes in the pet food. Regarding this point, several hot topics may be suggested (Table 1).

IV. CONCLUSION

The pet food industry may take advantage of an appropriate e-nose and e-tongue system as a powerful tool for both quality control and research & development purposes. Future work is needed on the materials' side (sensors' array), on the data analysis side (better modelling, development of data fusion analysis for the process control system for a continuous quality assurance), and on the industrial side (better understanding of the industrial needs related to quality control and monitoring of food processing). Moreover, to develop the full potential of an electronic sense analysis of pet food, e-nose and e-tongue could be integrated in an instrumental platform including electronic sensors for colour, texture, size, and shape evaluation. Once properly set, this platform could replace animal preference test, chemical and texture analysis to assess pet food palatability.

REFERENCES

[1] K. Koppel, "Sensory analysis of pet foods," Journal of the Science of Food and Agriculture, vol 94, pp. 2148-2153, March 2014, doi:10.1002/jsfa.6597.

[2] G. C. Aldrich and K. Koppel, "Pet Food Palatability Evaluation: A Review of Standard Assay Techniques and Interpretation of Results with a Primary Focus on Limitations," Animals, vol 5, pp. 43-55, May 2015, doi:10.3390/ani5010043.

[3] B. Di Donfrancesco, K. Koppel, and E. Chambers IV, "An initial lexicon for sensory properties of dry dog food," Journal of Sensory Studies, vol 27, pp. 498-510, December 2012, doi:10.1111/joss.12017.

[4] K. Koppel, K. Adhikari, and B. Di Donfrancesco, "Volatile Compounds in Dry Dog Foods and Their Influence on Sensory Aromatic Profile," Molecules, vol 18, pp 2646-2662, March 2013, doi:10.3390/molecules18032646.

[5] F. Cheli, A. Campagnoli, L. Pinotti, F. D'Ambrosio, and A. Crotti, "Electronic nose application in animal protein sources characterisation in pet food," Proc. LXI Annual Meeting of the Italian Society for Veterinary Science, pp. 26-29, September 2007.

[6] B. Oladipupo, J. Stough, and N. Guthrie, "Application of combined electronic nose and tongue technology in petfood flavor development and quality control," AIP Conference Proc., May 2011, 1362, pp. 75-76, doi.org/10.1063/1.3626311.

[7] V. Éles, I. Hullár, and R. Romvári, "Electronic nose and tongue for pet food classification," Agriculturae Conspectus Scientificus, vol 78, pp. 225-228, September 2013.

[8] V. Éles et al., "Electronic nose for evaluating cat food quality," Proc. of the 16th International Symposium on olfaction and electronic nose, pp. 35-36, June 2015.

[9] D. Battaglia, M. Ottoboni, V. Caprarulo, L. Pinotti, and F. Cheli, "Electronic nose in commercial pet food evaluation". II International Congress Food Technology, Quality and Safety and XVI International Symposium Feed Technology, pp. 28-30, October 2014.

Design and Fabrication of Sensor Chip with Heater for Semiconductor Flip-Chip Package Application

Boo Taek Lim, Young-Su Kim, Nam Soo Park, Boung Ju Lee
Nano Device Development team
National NanoFab Center
Daejeon, Korea
email:btlim@nnfc.re.kr

***Abstract*— A heat generated from semiconductor chips and chip packages is considered a critical issue for high-performance and reliable device operation. In this paper we demonstrate a simple semiconductor chip with both heat generation and temperature sensor functions. By evaluating the relationship between the temperature of the chip and the resistance of the sensor, the thermal properties of the semiconductor package material can be determined. The heat generation block and temperature sensor are made of aluminum lines, not active circuit, so manufacturing cost is low and the processes are simple.**

Keywords- semiconductor; sensor chip; heater; micro-bump; flip-chip package; thermal reliability

I. INTRODUCTION

Due to increased complexity, integrity and operating speed, the heat generated by semiconductor chips and chip packages has been viewed as a problem to be solved for high performance and reliable device operation. The demand for diverse applications requiring small and high-speed operation, such as smartphones and wearable appliances, has dramatically increased heat generation. For this reason, testing and managing the heat of the chip has become very important in commercial devices [1], [2]. The packaging technology of integrated circuits has also been technologically advanced. As a way to solve the performance degradation problem due to the heat rise of the chip, the underfill material is used for the flip chip packaging technology.

In this paper, we propose and demonstrate a simple semiconductor chip with heat generation function and temperature sensor to test thermal characteristics of the packaging materials. This chip is much simpler than the diode temperature sensor array chip used to evaluate the thermal properties of semiconductor underfill materials and makes more profitable in terms of manufacturing cost and duration [3]. It was fabricated in National NanoFab Center (NNFC) of Korea using Complementary Metal Oxide semiconductor (CMOS) and Micro Electro Mechanical System (MEMS) manufacturing processes. The fabricated chips were characterized using an I-V measuring instrument and a temperature measuring instrument with a Thermo-Electric Couple (TEC) controller.

II. DESIGN AND FABRICATION

As shown in Figure 1, the heat generation area (heater) and the temperature sensing line (sensor) are integrated on a single chip at the same time. The heater block is placed on both sides of the sensor. Each heater block is designed for 200-ohm to generate heat. The sensor detects the temperature with a simple principle that the resistance increases when it receives heat, and it is designed 1K-ohm

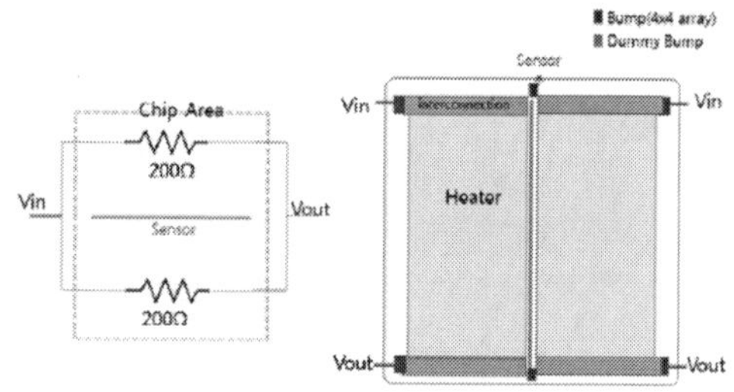

Figure 1. Schematic of chip with heater and sensor.

After deposit a protection layer and open the pad, the Sn/Ag micro-bump was formed on the chip pad with a diameter of 70um as shown in Figure 2.

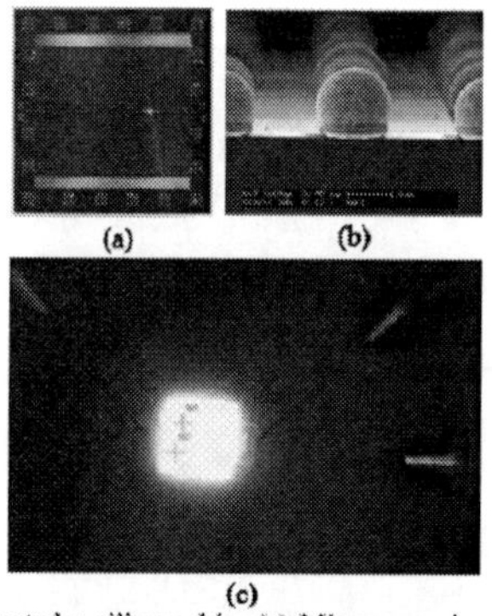

Figure 2. Fabricated a silicon chip. (a) Microscope image of chip, (b) Micro-bump array SEM image, (c) Thermal image of IR camera on flip chip packaged on PCB

The IR camera image shows that heat is generated when the heater block is powered up, as shown in Figure 2(c). When the underfill material is filled between the chip and the Printed Circuit Board (PCB), the generated heat is transferred to the PCB through the underfill material, so that the chip temperature does not rise. The chip temperature rise rate is determined by the thermal conductivity of the underfill material.

III. MEASUREMENT

The fabricated chip was characterized with I-V measuring instrument and temperature measuring instrument with TEC controller. First, the chip temperature is measured while increasing the applied voltage as shown Figure 3(a), then, the resistance of the sensor was measured in the same way as shown in Figure 3(b). When the power is supplied to the heater block, heat is generated in the 200-ohm aluminum line per block and chip temperature rises. The generated heat is transferred to the sensor located in the center of the chip, increasing the resistance of the sensor. It can be seen that as the voltage increases, the temperature of chip and the resistance of sensor increase with the shape of the quadratic function. Based on these results, the resistance of the sensor versus temperature of the chip is derived as shown in Figure 3(c). Using this result, the temperature of chip can be determined by measuring the resistance of the sensor without measuring directly with the thermometer.

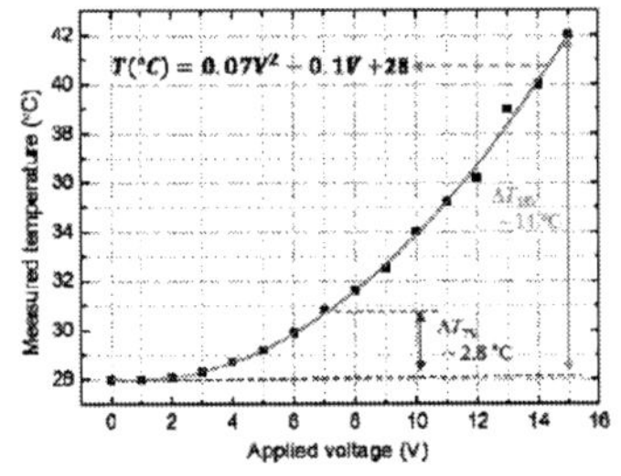

(a)

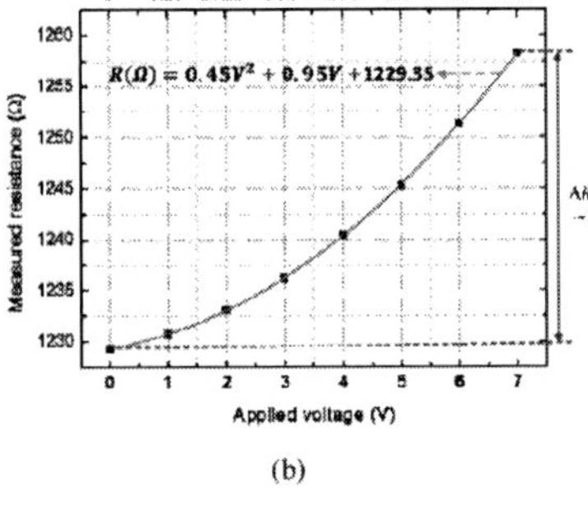

(b)

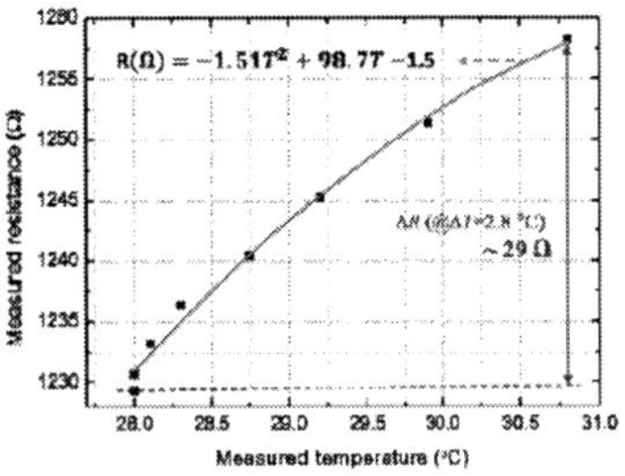

(c)

Figure 3. Electrical characteristics of the proposed chip. (a) Measured resistance of sensor, (b) Measured temperature of chip, (c) Calculated resistance as a function of temperature.

This result is very useful for testing semiconductor packaging materials such as underfill. Unerfill fills the gap between the chip and PCB for heat transfer and bump protection. The higher the thermal conductivity of the underfill material, the more heat is transferred to the PCB. As a result, the temperature of the chip and the resistance of the sensor will not increase significantly.

IV. CONCLUSION

We have demonstrated the relationship between chip temperature and sensor resistance by fabricating chip with heat generation and thermal sensor functionality using semiconductor processes. The proposed structure and method can be used to test the thermal properties of semiconductor packaging materials.

REFERENCES

[1] S. Ali, K. Sung-Mo, B. Avran, and C. Bernad, "Scanning the special issue on on-chip thermal engineering," *Proc. IEEE*, vol. 94, no. 8 , pp. 1473-1475, 2006.

[2] M. Toshihiro, D. Haruka, and I. Hideyuki, "Tomoyuki H., Takashi, O. A test structure for analysis of metal wire effect on temperature distribution in stacked IC," *Int. C. Microelectronic Test Structure (ICMTS)*, 2-1, pp.22-26, 2016.

[3] Lee. W.S, Han. I.Y, Yu. Jin, Kim. S.J, and Byun. K.Y, "Thermal characterization of thermally conductive underfil for a flip-chip package using novel temperature sensing technoque," Thermochinica Acta 455, 148-155, 2007.

Using the Measurement-Based Approach to Emulate the Behavior of a Sensor for Internal Hydraulic Pressure Drop Measurements of Sprayers in the Agricultural Industry

Rafael F. Q. Magossi[1,2], Elmer A. G. Peñaloza[1,2], Shankar P. Battachharya [3], Vilma A. Oliveira[2], Paulo E. Cruvinel[1]

[1]Embrapa Instrumentation
Brazilian Agricultural Research Corporation, São Carlos, SP, Brazil
Email: paulo.cruvinel@embrapa.br

[2] Department of Electrical and Computer Engineering
Universidade de São Paulo, São Carlos, SP, Brazil
Email: rafael.magossi, egamboa@usp.br, vilma@sc.usp.br

[3]Department of Electrical and Computer Engineering
Texas A&M University, College Station, Texas, USA
Email: bhatt@ece.tamu.edu

Abstract—**Related to the quality of the agricultural spraying processes, the variable hydraulic pressure plays an important role. All spray nozzles when operating are subjected to the hydraulic pressure along the boom. Furthermore, in real sprayers systems the losses in the hydraulic pressure which occur along the boom, where one may find the placed nozzles, are in general verified with the use of pressure sensors in each nozzle. However, such arrangement has high costs for the agricultural producers and involves a larger complexity in the electronics for signal processing, monitoring and control. The hydraulic system of agricultural sprayers has a direct analog in electric circuits, and thus, it is possible to be represented as an equivalent circuit formed by a voltage source and a resistance which characterizes the internal loss of the system. This paper, presents a method that makes possible the evaluation of the hydraulic pressure drop in bars of sprayer systems considering the fluid hydraulic resistance as a part of a sensor element, associated with a point-wise Thévenin's equivalent measurement method. This makes feasible such evaluations with lower cost and greater accuracy, as well as the control of the pressure drop. Thus, taking into account a metering-based approach it was possible to obtain a parametrized relationship among operating conditions and fluid resistances. Therefore, it was possible to obtain the hydraulic equivalent of a sprayer system with direct injection based only on the hydraulic flow and pressure measurements. The results have shown that is possible to get the hydraulic equivalent resistance with a relative error equal to 2.1529%.**

Keywords–Metering; Measurement theory; Parametrized model; Pointwise Thévenin's equivalent; Electrical-hydraulic analogy; Agricultural quality sensor.

I. INTRODUCTION

Today, hydraulic systems can be found in a wide variety of applications, also in agriculture. For such systems it is important the determination of the internal losses occurring not only for the establishment of valves' upstream and downstream pressure but also to calculate the flow rates through piping systems. Additionally, such information can help in the establishment of the flow rate range, associated with the design and size of the pumps, compressors, turbines and the relief headers to ensure that back pressure on the relief devices not preventing them from functioning properly [1].

The fluid hydraulic resistance is a function of the flow regime, therefore being dependent of the Reynolds number and the relative pipe. The Reynolds number for pipes, in turn, is a function of the velocity (m/s), density (kg/m^3), and viscosity ($Pa \cdot s$) of the fluid, as well as of their internal diameters. Since the temperature also affects the Reynolds number, it becomes important to take that into account when one is working with sprayers systems [2], [3]. Besides, the fluid hydraulic resistance is subject to temporal variations, and requires considerable effort for its determination. In this scenario a sensor that can measure the internal losses of the hydraulic boom pressure in sprayers is very much required.

Pesticide application is a vital component for food security, whose production is directly connected to pest control. Sprayer is the machine used to apply liquid chemicals on plants to control pest and diseases. In addition, it can be used to apply herbicides to control weeds and to spray micro nutrients to enhance plants growth. There are many types of sprayer's commercially available for producers and they are designed for its own particular duties and use. Regarding to such matter one may find backpack sprayers, hand compression sprayers, self-propelled sprayers and pull-behind sprayers, among others.

The manual application method was the first to be used in agriculture, but they have the disadvantage to present a higher risk to the human resources. On the other hand, turning off sprayers when there is no target, or adjusting application rates based on canopy size and density became to be essential for production with sustainability, i.e., in such matter the automated sprayers play an important role. Close to the 90 decade, manufacturers introduced precision spraying technology in boom sprayers [4]. Despite being still an open field for research and innovation, in this direction the variable rate methods, using the Global Position System (GPS) and the Geographic

Information System (GIS) technologies were integrated into boom sprayers and became already commercially available.

The GPS and GIS have been popularized and the combination of these two technologies allowed the diffusion of Precision Agriculture (PA) in the entire world. The PA brings together the use of technologies for the management of soil, inputs and crops, in a manner appropriate to the spatial and temporal variations in factors, which affect their productivity, in order to increase efficiency.

The adoption of PA for localized application of agrochemicals can reduce pesticide wastage and environmental aggression, providing a more efficient production of large-scale food and increasing agricultural productivity. With localized application of agrochemicals, herbicide savings is in the order of 30 to 80% compared to the uniform application in the total area. Automatic sprayers designed and developed for localized application are currently available, allowing the use of large volume of syrup, covering large agricultural areas [5]–[8].

In this field of knowledge, there are the use of conventional and direct injection sprayers system. The first type of direct injection system was developed between the 70's and 80's decades. However in that time such a system presented high cost, complexity of operation and low performance. According to Baio and Antuniassi [7], the main characteristic of direct injection systems is related to the storage of the diluent (water) and the pesticide in separate containers.

The mixing is carried out only at the time of application, by injection of the pesticide into the piping, which carries the syrup to the nozzles of the sprayer. The amount of injected pesticide can be accomplished, among other ways, by controlling the rotation of the piston or peristaltic injection pumps. The main advantages of the injection system are the reduction of risks involved during the application process [9].

Other aspects one should be taken into account, in relation to this matter, is the benefit/cost rate is terms of the use of energy in the agricultural machinery. The success of agriculture, manufacturing, transportation, military systems and construction machinery owes much to the efficient use of fluid energy. Most fluid energy systems are configured with a positive flow displacement pump that is large enough to meet the flow requirements of many circuits. Different work functions require a variety of flow and pressure values to provide the desired operation. Branches of the system therefore must include specific flow and pressure regulating valves.

In the process of agricultural spraying, it is of great importance to know the value of the fluid resistance of the spray boom since, variations in this resistance can affect the quality of the application, i.e., size and volume of drops, distribution of drops on the crop and the drift of the drops produced by the wind [10]. Droplet size and distribution are critical factors in such processes because can be affected the penetration, coverage and drift of the application on the crop [11].

The design of a hydraulic system can be improved with the use of mathematical simulation. Numerous approaches to energy systems modeling fluids and components, can be found in the literature. Analysis of a fluid feed system can cover the flow distribution, the functioning of components, or a combination of both. Most of the useful equations for fluid analysis are derived from the law of conservation of energy, the principle of continuity, and Newton's second law [12].

Equations used to calculate flow in circuits involve the use of empirical expressions or laboratory-derived flow coefficients. Therefore, when two or more circuits are used simultaneously, the principle of continuity may not be obeyed exactly, because of the use of such empirical coefficients. To model a flow regulating valve, a good medium must also be used to define how the flow divides in the active circuit branches.

Usually, this is done by writing a set of equations to determine the desired pressure and flow values, which can be solved via an iterative method. Iterative methods work well for steady state flow conditions, however, they are difficult to apply to non-steady state operations. In relation to such subject Akers and collaborators have shown a method based on electrical-hydraulic analogy was proposed [2]. In this method, fluid pressure, flow, and flow resistance are analogous to voltage, current, and electrical resistance, respectively. The method uses the basic principle of the Ohm's law, also referred to as the hydraulic Ohm.

On the other hand, a fluid moves inside a pipe occurs a fluid friction with the inner walls of this pipe and a turbulence of the fluid with itself. This phenomenon causes the pressure inside the pipe to gradually decrease as the fluid moves and the pressure decrease is known as the pressure drop. In this way, the load loss would be related to a resistance to the passage of the flow of the fluid inside the pipe, this resistance is known as fluid resistance and affects directly the monomeric height of a pump denoted H and its volumetric flow denoted Q. The pressure (p) can be related to the volumetric flow rate by:

$$p = f_a \frac{L\rho}{2DA^2} Q^2 \tag{1}$$

for a rough pipe with turbulent flow or:

$$p = \frac{8\pi L\mu}{A^2} Q^2 \tag{2}$$

for a flat tube with laminar flow, where f_a is the coefficient of friction [dimensionless], ρ is the specific mass of the fluid $[kg/m^3]$, L is the equivalent pipe length $[m]$, D is the internal diameter of the pipe $[m]$, A is the inner area of the straight section of the pipe $[m^2]$ and μ is the absolute viscosity of the fluid $[P_a \cdot s]$.

The coefficient of friction f_a, sometimes known as a Moody friction factor or also as a distributed load loss coefficient determined by mathematical equations, is a function of the Reynolds number (Re) and relative roughness. Experimental identification of f_a is more common due to the non linear characteristics involved. For pipes that undergo changes in pipe diameters, in general, flow type or over-curves, fluid resistance may be related to the remainder of the fluid system by:

$$\sqrt{\Delta P} = RQ \tag{3}$$

where ΔP is the pressure drop across the hydraulic element and R is the fluid resistance. For a tube, the fluid resistance is given by:

$$R = \sqrt{f_a \frac{L\rho}{2DA^2}}. \tag{4}$$

For a hole, the fluid resistance is given by:

$$R = \sqrt{\frac{\rho}{2}\frac{1}{C_d A}} \tag{5}$$

where C_d is the discharge coefficient [unit-less].

The next sections of the paper are organized as follows. In Section II, the methodology used to obtain the function relating the hole diameter with the flow in a nozzle is given. In Section III, an experimental validation of the pointwise Thévenin's equivalent and the nozzle flow using a laboratory sprayer setup is performed. Finally, some concluding remarks are presented in Section IV.

II. METHODOLOGY

The well known Thévenin's equivalent circuit of a linear circuit is composed of an equivalent impedance and voltage, which for some cases are organized just with a resistor and a source of continuous voltage. This equivalent circuit is obtained through Thévenin's Theorem:

Theorem 1 (Thévenin's Theorem):

$$V_{th} = V_{oc} \tag{6}$$

$$R_{th} = \frac{V_{oc}}{I_{sc}} \tag{7}$$

where I_{sc} is the short-circuit current and V_{oc} the open circuit voltage [13]–[16].

The Thévenin's equivalent circuit can be represented by Fig 1. In Fig. 1, the voltage and current are described by:

$$I = \frac{V_{th}}{R_{th} + R} \tag{8}$$

$$V = RI = -R_{th}I + V_{th}. \tag{9}$$

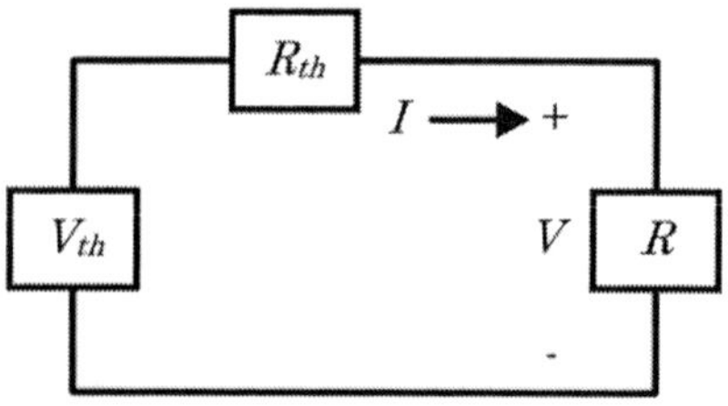

Figure 1. Thévenin's equivalent circuit.

Let $y(1)$ and $y(2)$ denote current measurements taken with values of load R in Fig. 1 for $R(1)$ and $R(2)$, respectively. According to Bhattacharyya and collaborators [17] and Mohsenizadeh and collaborators [18], the Thévenin's equivalent can also be obtained by solving the linear equation system, in terms of α_0 and β_0:

$$\begin{pmatrix} y(1) & -1 \\ y(2) & -1 \end{pmatrix}\begin{pmatrix} \alpha_0 \\ \beta_0 \end{pmatrix} = \begin{pmatrix} -y(1)R(1) \\ -y(2)R(2) \end{pmatrix} \tag{10}$$

where α_0 and β_0 are given by:

$$\alpha_0 = R_{th} \tag{11}$$

$$\beta_0 = V_{th}. \tag{12}$$

if one is considering a linear characteristic then is possible to write:

$$V_{oc} = V_{th} \tag{13}$$

$$I_{sc} = \frac{V_{th}}{R_{th}}. \tag{14}$$

Otherwise, one can consider, as a further step, the electric analog already described in Section I, then $V = \sqrt{\Delta p}$ e $V_{th} = \sqrt{\Delta p_{th}}$. Now, let $y(1)$ e $y(2)$ be a measure of flow in the boom with the nozzles of interest, where $R(1)$ and $R(2)$ correspond to the equivalent fluid resistance of the nozzles of the boom of interest, thus:

$$\begin{pmatrix} Q(1) & -1 \\ Q(2) & -1 \end{pmatrix}\begin{pmatrix} \alpha_0 \\ \beta_0 \end{pmatrix} = \begin{pmatrix} -\sqrt{\Delta p}(1) \\ -\sqrt{\Delta p}(2) \end{pmatrix} \tag{15}$$

where α_0 e β_0 are given by:

$$\alpha_0 = R_{th} \tag{16}$$

$$\beta_0 = \Delta p_{th}. \tag{17}$$

where R_{th} and Δp_{th} are the internal loss equivalent and the internal pressure equivalent, respectively. As the behavior of pressure and flow is non-linear, then there will be more than one possible representation of the Thévenin's equivalent. If the measurements are taken as close as possible to each other, it is then said that a pointwise Thévenin's equivalent is obtained.

It is known that the flow in a nozzle is a function of the hole diameter denoted d, pressure and other hydraulic parameters, which may change with different types of nozzle. Then, it is possible to find a function which relates the hole diameter with the flow in a nozzle. If consider the rank in relation to parameter d and pressure p of the matrices appearing in the description of the flow Q as one, again according with Bhattacharyya and collaborators [17] it is possible to find:

$$Q = \frac{\beta_0 + \beta_1 d + \beta_2 p + \beta_3 dp}{\alpha_0 + \alpha_1 d + \alpha_2 p + dp} \tag{18}$$

where $\beta_0, \beta_1, \beta_2, \beta_3, \alpha_0, \alpha_1$ and α_2 are constants and $(\alpha_0 + \alpha_1 d + \alpha_2 p + dp) \neq 0$. To find these constants, one should take just 7 measurements with different values of d and p and solve the following linear system:

$$\begin{bmatrix} 1 & d(1) & p(1) & d(1)p(1) & -Q(1) & -Q(1)d(1) & -Q(1)p(1) \\ 1 & d(2) & p(2) & d(2)p(2) & -Q(2) & -Q(2)d(2) & -Q(2)p(2) \\ 1 & d(3) & p(3) & d(3)p(3) & -Q(3) & -Q(3)d(3) & -Q(3)p(3) \\ 1 & d(4) & p(4) & d(4)p(4) & -Q(4) & -Q(4)d(4) & -Q(4)p(4) \\ 1 & d(5) & p(5) & d(5)p(5) & -Q(5) & -Q(5)d(5) & -Q(5)p(5) \\ 1 & d(6) & p(6) & d(6)p(6) & -Q(6) & -Q(6)d(6) & -Q(6)p(6) \\ 1 & d(7) & p(7) & d(7)p(7) & -Q(7) & -Q(7)d(7) & -Q(7)p(7) \end{bmatrix} \begin{bmatrix} \beta_0 \\ \beta_1 \\ \beta_2 \\ \beta_3 \\ \alpha_0 \\ \alpha_1 \\ \alpha_2 \end{bmatrix} = \begin{bmatrix} Q(1)d(1)p(1) \\ Q(2)d(2)p(2) \\ Q(3)d(3)p(3) \\ Q(4)d(4)p(4) \\ Q(5)d(5)p(5) \\ Q(6)d(6)p(6) \\ Q(7)d(7)p(7) \end{bmatrix}. \tag{19}$$

III. Experimental Validation

The Agricultural Sprayer Development System (SDPA) used is located at the Laboratory of Agricultural Precision Spraying of the Embrapa Instrumentation (Fig. 2) in São Carlos, SP, Brazil [9], [19], [20]. The goal is to obtain linear pressure and fluid resistance equivalent by selecting a boom with nozzles of interest using regular measurements. This is possible by solving (10).

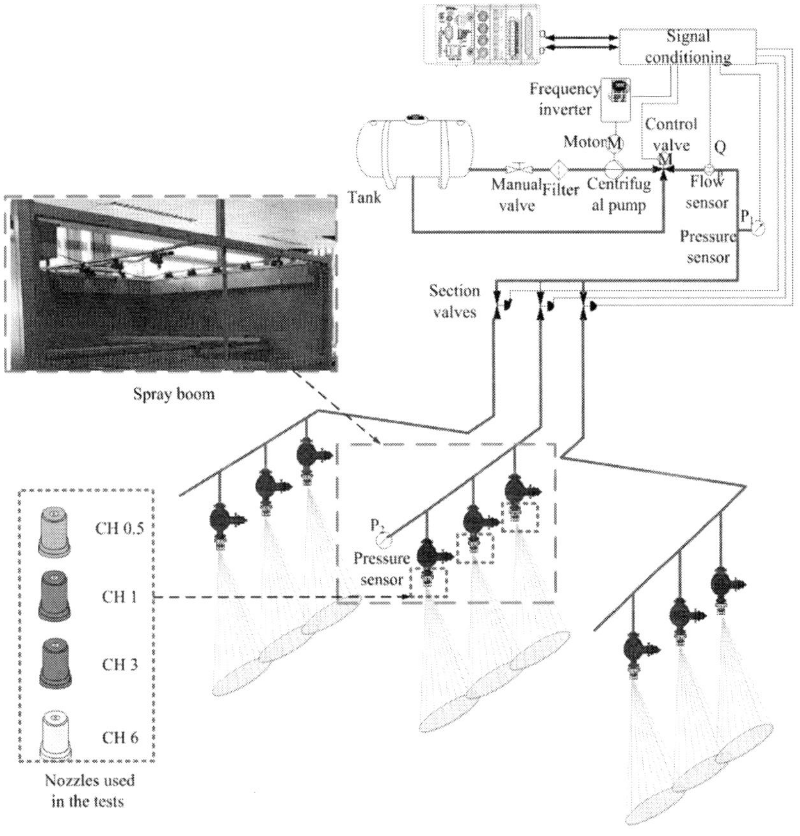

Figure 2. Hydraulic and electrical configuration of the SDPA for testing and validation.

A. *Thévenin's Equivalent Validation*

To obtain the hydraulic Thevenin equivalent, according to the proposed methodology, only two different fluid resistances are required. However, it is necessary that when the fluid resistance changes, a significant variation of pressure and flow occurs at the point of interest. Otherwise, if any of these measures are kept constant, the equivalent will have the trivial solution.

As the pressure is regulated in the system, a pressure variation of approximately 0.1 bar was considered significant because of the inherent noise of the spray sensors. The objective is to extract the Thévenin's equivalent of the central sprayer boom which is also shown in Fig. 2. All nozzles of the central spray boom are of type CH05.

1) Measurements set up: Each sprayer boom has 3 spray nozzles. First, the pump pressure was set at 3.5 bar and the pressure at the center boom spray nozzles was found to be about 3.48 bar. After this verification, just one nozzle was changed to type CH3. The pressure in the spray nozzles rose to 3.47 bar and was therefore considered as noise. Another attempt was made on in the same nozzle that was replaced by a nozzle type CH6 (which allows the greatest possible flow between the nozzles of this line). The pressure in the nozzles rose to 3.46 and was again considered as noise. Two nozzle were then replaced by CH3 type nozzles and the pressure in the spray nozzles was found to be 3.44 bar, also considered to be noise. In this way, all the nozzles of the central bar were changed to type CH3 and the pressure in that time was equal to 3.39 bar. This pressure drop was then considered as significant and thus concluding that for the system to stop regulating the pressure in the bar it became necessary to change all the nozzles of the bar.

To extract the Thévenin's equivalent, only two different nozzles are required. However, to validate the obtained equivalent, three nozzles were used, where the third nozzle has an intermediate fluid resistance between the other two nozzles used for extraction of the equivalent. Then, the nozzles of the central boom were changed in the row of full cone nozzles and the pressure and flow measurements taken. The data are shown in Table I.

2) Results: Using (15), the following equivalent was obtained:

$$\Delta P_{th} = 3.4394\ [bar]$$
$$R_{th} = 0.0649\ [bar \cdot min \cdot L^{-1}].$$

TABLE I. DATA OBTAINED FOR DIFFERENT FULL CONE NOZZLES

Nozzles	Pressure [bar]	Flow [L/min]
CH05	3.4046	0.535
CH3	3.3491	1.420
CH6	3.2946	2.230

Thus, this equivalent was used to estimate the flow of arbitrary pressure values. The result is shown in Fig. 3. The error of estimated flow is 2.1529%.

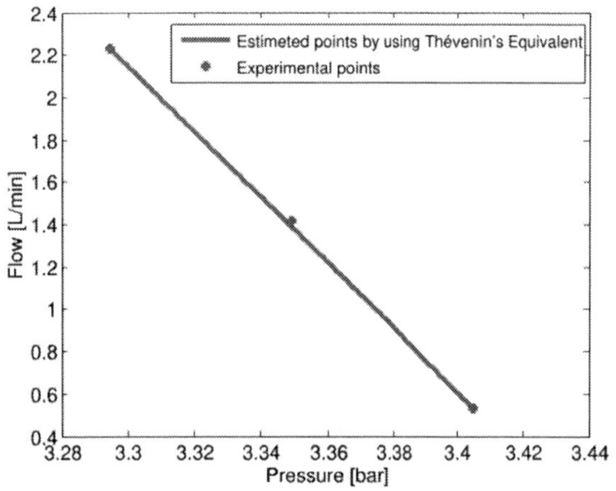

Figure 3. Thevenin equivalent for full cone nozzles.

B. Nozzle Flow Validation

To validate (18) which relates the flow to the hole diameter, a single nozzle was used. The datasheet of a nozzle MAG CH, produced by MAGNOJET®, was used. There it is possible find the values of pressure and flow for each nozzle. The hole diameter was measured using a pachymeter. The 7 points shown in Table II were selected, which cover all the producer table, and were used to solve the linear system (19). With the solution of (19), it was possible to generate the surface shown in Fig. 4.

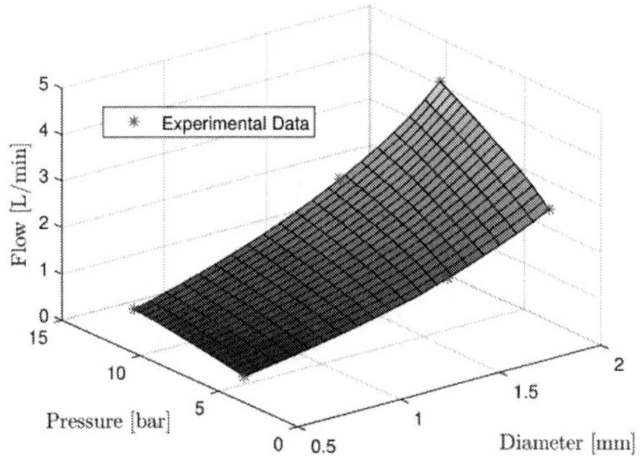

Figure 4. Surface relating the hole diameter d and the pressure with the output flow for the full cone nozzle.

TABLE II. SELECTED MEASUREMENTS FROM THE MAGNOJET PRODUCER DATASHEET.

Nozzle	Pressure [bar]	Q [L/min]	d [mm]
CH05	3.4	0.56	0.5
CH3	3.4	1.5	1.5
CH6	3.4	2.4	2
CH05	10.4	0.94	0.5
CH3	10.4	2.55	1.5
CH6	10.4	4.08	2
CH3	7.6	2.2	1.5

Now, it is possible to predict the flow of the nozzle given the diameter of the hole and the pressure in the nozzle. In Table III, there are shown the results of a prediction using the nozzle CH1.

TABLE III. PREDICTED FLOW AND THE CATALOG FLOW TO CH1 NOZZLE USING THE SURFACE

Pressure [bar]	d [mm]	Predicted flow [L/min]	Catalog Flow [L/min]	Relative error [%]
3.4	1	0.94	1	5.90
4.8	1	1.10	1.2	8.00
6.2	1	1.25	1.33	6.17
7.6	1	1.38	1.47	6.39
9	1	1.49	1.63	8.54
10.4	1	1.60	1.74	8.39

By comparing the prediction given by (18) to the flow provided in the manufacturer's catalog, an average relative error around 7% can be found, which is an acceptable error considering all the involved parameters.

IV. CONCLUSION

In this paper, the measurement-based approach was used to emulate the behavior of a sensor to allow the quality analyses of direct injection sprayers. With few measurements, the fluid resistance equivalent of a piping system was obtained. In addiction, a flow function of a full cone nozzle relating the nozzle internal diameter and pressure were estimated. The results obtained were satisfactory and the extension of this work includes the hardware implementation of the sensor and the application of the measurement-based approach to quality control of spray droplets in agriculture.

ACKNOWLEDGMENT

This work was supported by the Brazilian Agricultural Research Corporation - Embrapa (grant numbers MP2 - 02.11.07.025.00.00, MP1 - 01.14.09.001.05.05); the National Counsel of Technological and Scientific Development - CNPq (grant number 306.477/2013-0). The authors also thank the MAGNOJET® by the availability of the nozzles for validation of the developed method.

REFERENCES

[1] R. Mulley, *Flow of industrial fluids: theory and equations*. CRC Press, 2004.

[2] A. Akers, M. Gassman, and R. Smith, *Hydraulic Power System Analysis*. Broken Sound Parkway: CRC Press, 2006.

[3] J. xian Zhang, Y. tao Ju, S. qiang Zhou, and C. Zhou, "Air-pasty propellant pressure drop and heat transfer through round pipe," in *2008 Asia Simulation Conference - 7th International Conference on System Simulation and Scientific Computing*, Oct 2008, pp. 1282–1285.

[4] L. E. Bode and S. M. Bretthauer, "Agricultural chemical application technology: a remarkable past and an amazing future," *Transactions of the ASAE (American Society of Agricultural Engineers)*, vol. 51, no. 2, p. 391, 2008.

[5] P. Chueca, C. Garcera, E. Molto, and A. Gutierrez, "Development of a sensor-controlled sprayer for applying low-volume bait treatments," *Crop Protection*, vol. 27, no. 10, pp. 1373–1379, 2008.

[6] S. Han, L. L. Hendrickson, B. Ni, and Q. Zhang, "Modification and testing of a comercial sprayer with pwm solenoids for precision spraying," *Applied Engineering in Agriculture*, vol. 5, no. 17, pp. 591–594, 2001.

[7] F. H. R. Baio and U. R. Antuniassi, "Sistemas de controle eletrônico e navegação para pulverizadores (electronic control and navigation systems for sprayers)," in *Tecnologia de Aplicação para Culturas Anuais (Application Technology for Annual Crops)*, U. R. Antuniassi and W. Boller, Eds. Passo Fundo: Aldeia Norte, 2011.

[8] P. E. Cruvinel, D. Karam, and M. G. Beraldo, "Method for the precision application of herbicides in the controlling of weed species into a culture of maize," in *VII Simpósio Internacional de Tecnologia de Aplicação (International Symposium on Application Technology)*. Uberlândia,MG: SINTAG, 2015.

[9] K. R. Felizardo, H. V. Mercaldi, P. E. Cruvinel, V. A. Oliveira, and B. L. Steward, "Modeling and model validation of a chemical injection sprayer system," *Applied Engineering in Agriculture*, vol. 32, no. 3, pp. 285–297, 2016.

[10] Y. Suzumura and P. E. Cruvinel, "Análise de qualidade da eficiência da pulverização agrícola com processamento de imagem e rede neural (quality analysis of crop spray efficiency with image processing and neural network)," *Sinergia*, vol. 6, no. 2, pp. 129–137, 2005.

[11] R. A. Kohl, "Drop size distribution from medium-sized agricultural sprinklers," *Transaction of the ASAE*, vol. 17, no. 4, pp. 690 – 693, 1974.

[12] P. A. Tipler and G. Mosca, *Physics for Scientists and Engineers*, 6th ed. New York: W. H. Freeman, 2007.

[13] L. Thévenin, "Extension de la loi d'ohm aux circuits électromoteurs complexes (extension of ohm's law to complex electromotive circuits)," *C. R. des Séances de l'Academie des Sciences*, 1883.

[14] L. Thévenin, "Sur un nouveau théorème d'électricité dynamique (on a new theorem of dynamic electricity)," *Annales Télégraphiques*, 1883.

[15] J. Brittain, "Thevenin's theorem," *Spectrum, IEEE*, vol. 27, no. 3, pp. 42–, 1990.

[16] D. Johnson, "Origins of the equivalent circuit concept: the current-source equivalent," *Proceedings of the IEEE*, vol. 91, no. 5, pp. 817–821, 2003.

[17] S. P. Bhattacharyya, L. H. Keel, and D. Mohsenizadeh, *Linear Systems: A Measurement Based Approach*, ser. Springer Briefs in Applied Sciences and Technology. Springer, 2013.

[18] N. Mohsenizadeh, H. Nounou, M. Nounou, A. Datta, and S. P. Bhattacharyya, "Linear circuits: a measurement-based approach," *International Journal of Circuit Theory and Applications*, vol. 43, no. 2, pp. 205–232, 2013.

[19] P. E. Cruvinel, V. A. Oliveira, K. R. Felizardo, and H. V. Mercaldi, "Bancada automatizada para ensaios e desenvolvimento de pulverizadores de agrotóxicos, aplicadores de fertilizantes líquidos e maturadores em culturas agrícolas sob manejo baseado em agricultura de precisão (automated bench for testing and development of pesticide sprays, liquid fertilizer applicators and ripeners in agricultural crops under precision agriculture based management)," in *Agricultura de Precisão: um Novo Olhar*. São Carlos, SP: Embrapa Instrumentação, 2011, pp. 96–100.

[20] P. E. Cruvinel, V. A. Oliveira, H. V. Mercaldi, E. A. G. Peñaloza, and K. R. Felizardo, "An advanced sensors-based platform for the development of agricultural sprayers," in *Sensors and Applications in Measuring and Automation Control Systems*, S. Y. Yurish, Ed. International Frequency Sensor Association, December 2016, pp. 181–204.

Low-cost Gas Concentration Sensor System

Multi-sensor package for industrial application

Axel Kramer, Teresa Jorge, Mariya Porus, Thomas Alfred Paul
Corporate Research - ABB Switzerland Ltd
5405 Baden-Dättwil, Switzerland
email: axel.kramer@ch.abb.com

Dieter Zeisel
Trafag AG
8608 Bubikon, Switzerland
email: dieter.zeisel@trafag.com

***Abstract*—We developed a novel multi-sensor system for online measurement of the composition of a binary gas mixture. The system provides information about pressure, temperature and density from which the partial pressure (or concentration) of the individual gas components in the mixture can be deduced. The sensors are housed in a small, robust package allowing the application in harsh industrial environments. In order to achieve highly precise information about the gas concentration, the sensor system is factory calibrated using a sophisticated calibration procedure. We report both on the procedure and theory used for calibration and on the experimental setup and procedure to validate the sensor system using certified gas mixtures. Moreover, the temperature effect on the concentration output was analyzed. We demonstrate, that our sensor can keep the concentration uncertainty as low as $\Delta c/c$ < ±2.5% over a temperature range of 10°C < T < 30°C.**

Keywords-Gas analyzer; binary mixture; composition sensor; density sensor; multi-sensor system; concentration measurement.

I. INTRODUCTION

In various industrial areas, the proportion of a component in a gas mixture must be known for efficient, reliable and safe operation. Here, we target the concentration determination of the various components in a novel electrical insulation gas [1][2]. For our and many other applications, laboratory analysis of the gas, e.g., by gas chromatography or spectroscopy, would be disadvantageous, since this is too complex and time consuming. Alternatives to these high-end solutions are, for example, systems based on acoustic sensing principles [3][4], on thermal measurements [5], or on damping effects of resonant mechanical oscillators [1][6]-[9]. Typically, the commercially available analyzers among these alternatives are expensive (4-10k USD, e.g., the binary gas analyzer BGA244 from Stanford Research or the MassSense® gas density meter (GDM) from ISS Inc.). However, for direct online surveillance of multiple locations in a facility, a more compact and more economic monitor solution based on a price level of ≈0.5k USD is preferred.

Here, we report on the development of such a low-cost sensor, its physical principle and its characterization. In section 2, the sensor concept, package, and the calibration procedure is outlined. In section 3, we present the results based on a gas mixture for a real application. Finally, in section 4, we discuss and conclude our achieved results.

II. SENSOR CONCEPT, PACKAGE AND CALIBRATION

The sensor principle is based on the measurement of pressure p, temperature T, and density ρ of the gas. The knowledge of these parameters enables us to determine the concentration in a binary gas mixture [6][7]. We emphasize that the concept is not limited to binary mixtures. It can be expanded to ternary and quaternary mixtures, as long as gas species of similar molar mass can be grouped (e.g., N_2 and O_2) [10]. The novelty of our work, reported here, lies in the realization of an industry-compatible sensor system that is low-cost, easy to use, and all sensors (p-T-ρ) and electronics (RS485 communication) are integrated into a robust stainless steel package (length < 90 mm, diameter ≤ 40 mm). In Fig. 1, the sensor (cipher 1) and an experimental test setup, used for sensor calibration, is shown. The peripheral devices, such as DAQ (NI, USB-X-Series 6341) and computer are not required for field application of the p-T-ρ sensor.

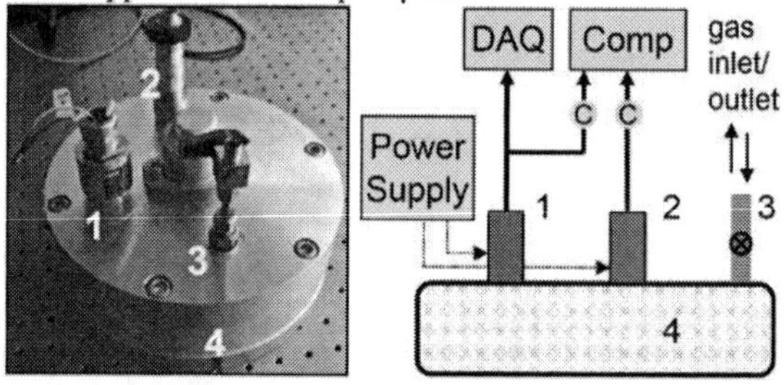

Figure 1. Setup for pressure and density calibration of the p-T-ρ sensor system. (1) p-T-ρ sensor, (2) Reference p-sensor for pressure calibration, (3) Gas inlet and outlet, (4) Pressure vessel of 1 dm³ volume.

The gas mixture we used for calibration (prefluoroketone $C_5F_{10}O$ (c = 34600 ppm) in nitrogen N_2) was purchased as a certified mixture with a relative concentration uncertainty of $\Delta c/c$ < ±1%. A calibration curve is shown in Fig. 2, relating the density ρ to the frequency f of the mechanical oscillator (our ρ-sensor) [9]. The density is calculated from measured p and T, using an appropriate equation of state for the used gas mixture [7]. During the calibration the pressure is varied and the temperature is fixed at 23.5°C. The calibration function is found by a least-squares fit of the model function [9] to the data, minimizing the sum of squared residuals (here, a residual being the relative difference between the measured value and the fitted value).

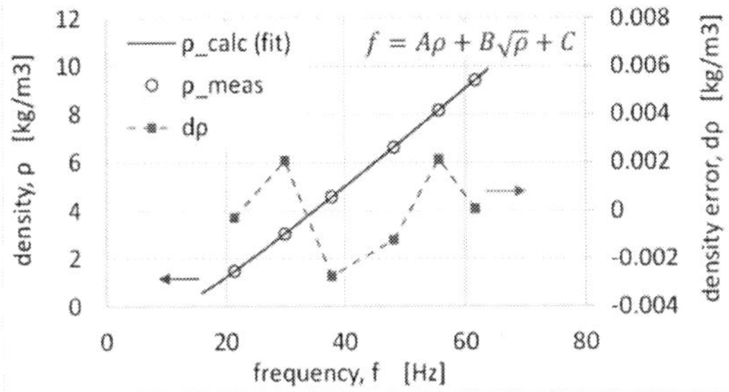

Figure 2. Density (ρ) – frequency (f) calibration curve (open circles: meas. data, full line: calibr. fct. fitted to data, (A, B, C) are fit parameters). Gas mixture: $C_5F_{10}O$: c=34'600 ppm, balanced by nitrogen.

It is evident from Fig. 2, that using this calibration method, the density uncertainty $d\rho$ can be reduced down to a few g/m^3.

III. RESULTS

After the calibration, the concentration sensor can be connected to any gas compartment. The concentration is then determined by an internal microprocessor based on the p-T-ρ method as described together with an uncertainty determination in [7]. Fig. 3 shows the result of a validation experiment, using in addition to the calibration gas (c = 34600 ppm) two certified gas mixtures of different concentrations. The sensor shows an accuracy of $\Delta c/c$ < ±1% for the calibration mixture. For the two other mixtures, the accuracy was $\Delta c/c$ < ±2.5% (Δc < ±900 ppm).

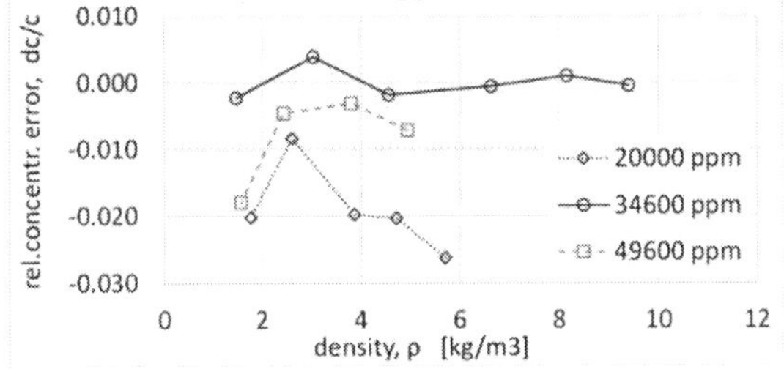

Figure 3. Validation test of the sensor for different gas mixtures (indicated is the concentration of $C_5F_{10}O$, balance gas is nitrogen).

We also investigated the temperature stability of our sensor system in the range between 10°C and 30°C (Fig. 4).

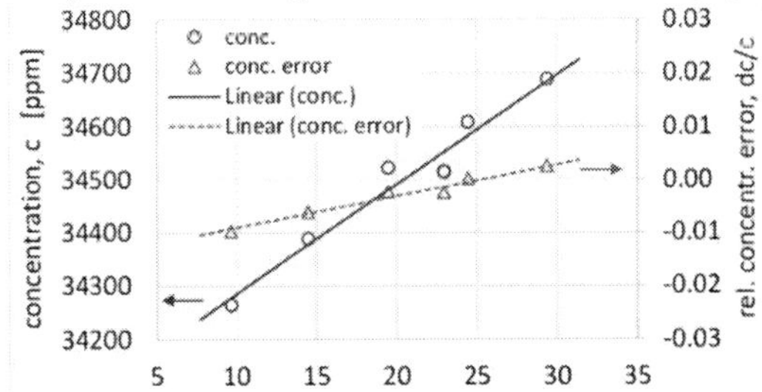

Figure 4. Temperature effect on concentration output (gas mixture: $C_5F_{10}O$: c=34'600 ppm, balanced by nitrogen).

As we can see from Fig. 4, the temperature effect on the sensor amounts to only dc/dT = 20 ppm/K or a relative concentration error of less than 1%.

IV. DISCUSSION AND CONCLUSION

To achieve our price target of <500 USD, we use cheap of-the-shelf articles. Although these individual sensors come with rather large uncertainties, we achieve a fairly high concentration accuracy due to our factory calibration. Of course, in order to keep production cost low, batch calibration of a multitude of sensors is envisaged. The accuracy of the competitor systems (section 1) are typically better by a factor of ten, however, they are not as compact as the one presented here and ten times more expensive. For various applications, it can be required to determine only a deviation from a set concentration. Calibrating at this target concentration, we have shown, that our sensor exhibits a relative uncertainty of less than 1%. For other concentrations, the uncertainty is slightly higher (2.5%). The reason for this might be the approximations, used to describe the equation of state and the mixing rules of the gas mixture.

In conclusion, our novel low-cost multi-sensor is integrated in a small and rugged package and is suitable for indoor industrial applications, e.g., online gas monitoring of insulation gas mixtures in electrical switchgear. In particular, our solution will be introduced further in pilot installations to leverage ABB's novel eco-friendly insulation gas.

REFERENCES

[1] M. Porus, A. Kramer, and T. A. Paul, "Application of a Multi-Parameter Sensor System for Monitoring Dielectric Insulation Gas Mixtures," IEEE Transactions on Dielectrics and Electrical Insulation, in press.

[2] A. Kramer, M. Porus, and T. A. Paul, "UV-LED based fiber-optic sensor system for gas analysis," in Conference on Lasers and Electro-Optics, OSA Technical Digest (online) (Optical Society of America, 2016), paper AM1J.5.

[3] L. Henn-Lecordier, J. N. Kidder, and G. W. Rubloff, "Real-time acoustic sensing and control of metalorganic chemical vapor deposition precursor concentrations delivered from solid phase sources," J. Vac. Sci. Technol., vol. A 22(5), pp.1984-1991, September/October 2004.

[4] L. Zisper, H. Franke, and W.-D. Bretschneider, "Acoustic sensors for analyzing binary gas mixtures," IEEE Sensors Journal, vol.6, pp.536-541, June 2006.

[5] C.J. Hepp, F.T. Krogmann, J. Polak, M.M. Lehmann, and G.A. Urban, "AC Characterisation of thermal flow sensor with fluid characterisation feature," 16th International Conference on Solid-State Sensors, Actuators and Microsystems, T3P.021 (2011) pp.1084-1087.

[6] O. Chetay, J.-P. Dupraz, L. Lucot, and D. Taponat, "Method and system of non-intrusively monitoring the mixture ratio of a gas mixture having at least two components," US Patent, US7184895 (B2), 2007.

[7] A. Kramer and T. A. Paul, "High-precision density sensor for concentration monitoring of binary gas mixtures," Sensors and Actuators A, vol. 202, pp. 52-56, 2013.

[8] D. Sparks, R. Smith, J. Patel, and N. Najafi, "A MEMS-based low pressure, light gas density and binary concentration sensor," Sens. and Actuators, vol. A 171, pp. 159-162, 2011.

[9] D. Zeisel, H. Menzi, and L. Ullrich, "A precise and robust quartz sensor based on tuning fork technology for SF_6-gas density control," Sens. and Actuat., vol. 80, pp. 233-236, 2000.

[10] A. Kramer, T. A. Paul, N. Mahdizadeh, and N. Ranjan, "Method and device for determining an operating parameter of a fluid insulated electrical apparatus," European patent EP2844998B1, 2015.

Optical Detection of Lesions in the Depth of a Solid Breast Phantom

Anett Bailleu, Axel Hagen, René Freyer
Hochschule für Technik und Wirtschaft Berlin
FB 1 – Energie und Information
12459 Berlin, Germany
e-mail: anett.bailleu@htw-berlin.de,
axel.hagen@htw-berlin.de, renefreyer@gmx.net

Dirk Grosenick
Physikalisch-Technische Bundesanstalt
PTB Berlin
10587 Berlin, Germany
e-mail: dirk.grosenick@ptb.de

Abstract— **In this study, a novel approach for optical imaging of tissue based on diffusely reflected photons was investigated. The examination object was an established solid breast phantom, which contains two absorbing lesions at different depths. The aim was to generate an absorption contrast image using depth discrimination to detect a lesion. The main questions was whether the required depth sensitivity is achievable with a near infrared line light source and a charge-coupled-device-camera. Different light sources were examined by comparative measurements. During the investigations observed speckle-effects could be reduced. The results of this study indicate that a translation of the approach from the breast phantom to in vivo studies appears feasible.**

Keywords— near infrared remission; optical tomography; deph sensitivity.

I. Introduction

Diffuse optical imaging is a powerful tool to gain physiological and functional information from healthy and diseased tissue [1]. With near-infrared radiation in the 650 nm to 1000 nm wavelength range tissue concentrations of characteristic absorbers such as oxygenated and deoxygenated hemoglobin can be determined non-invasively. Main applications of diffuse optical imaging include the detection and characterization of tumors, e.g.,, in the female breast [2], functional studies on the human brain [3] - [5], as well as tissue oxygenation measurements in muscles [6], [7]. Furthermore, contrast agents offer the possibility to exploit molecular signatures for early detection of diseases [8] - [19].

A challenging task in diffuse optical imaging is to obtain either fully three-dimensional images of tissue regions with high spatial resolution or, at least, depth-resolved information about the distribution of tissue absorbers of interest. Accordingly, different techniques have been developed such as 3D tomographic imaging, oblique projection imaging in transmission, time-resolved or spatially resolved detection of reflectance, as well as laminar optical tomography [20] - [22].

Currently our research group, Labor Prozessmess- und Stelltechnik at the Hochschule für Technik und Wirtschaft Berlin (HTW Berlin, university of applied science) with support from the Physikalisch-Technische Bundesanstalt Berlin (PTB, The National Metrology Institute of Germany), is developing a new procedure for near infrared (NIR) measurements [23] - [26], which has the potential to detect and depict changes in human tissue in a way suitable for medical diagnostics . This patented procedure [24] can complement and partly replace current radiologic imaging methods. This is desirable, since current technologies work with ionizing radiation and partly with radioactive markers (Scintigraphy-tracer), and therefore, additionally burden patients health.

Our proposed approach is a combination of two well-known methods: the light-section method (laser triangulation) [27] and the laminar optical tomography (LOT) [21], [22]. How it is possible to generate a 3D-scan by the light-section method in a very cost-effective way and how tomographic information of an examination object maybe combined with topographic information of the same object are subject-matters of other studies [23] - [26] and will not be described in this paper.

A. *Aim of the Study*

One of the most qualifying properties of the proposed procedure is the depth in which information can be obtained.

Fig. 1 shows a schematic representation of the LOT-principle. It depicts how to get optical information from inside of the examination object using a remission geometry.

A line generator and a light detector are placed at the same side of the examination object. The light source (a NIR-laser or NIR-light emission diode) projects a line on the surface of the examination object. A camera works as the light detector and takes images. The intensities of image-pixels in the vicinity of an "offset-line" are analyzed.

Measurements were carried out on an established solid-body phantom of a female breast in order to assess the depth sensitivity of the proposed procedure.

Extracted information of intrinsic absorbers from this mammary phantom are detected in both lateral and depth dimensions.

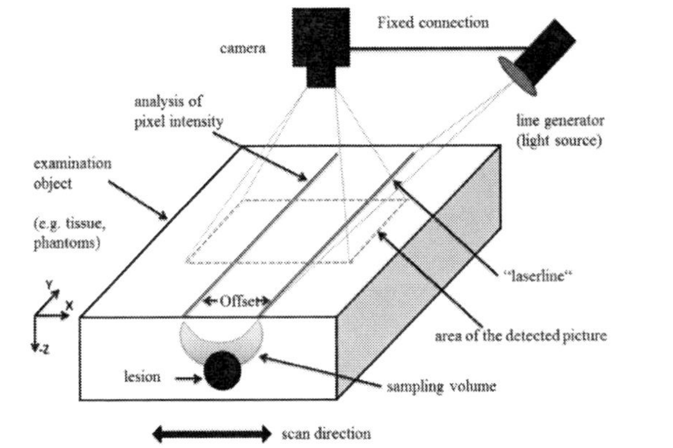

Figure 1. Principle to detect lesions in the sampled volume of a scattering examination object

B. *Structure of the paper*

The paper is divided into four main sections. Following the introduction in section 1, the section 2 contains a short description of the theoretical photon paths in a scattering medium as well as a description of the experimental setup and of the characteristics of the employed breast phantom. In section 3 measurement results are shown and interpreted. In section 4, the last one, we present a conclusion and an outlook into future work.

II. GENERATION OF DEPTH INFORMATION

The fundamentals of the investigation method are subdivided into a theoretical simulation and the experimental realization.

A. *Theoretical Model*

To gather information from the depth of a scattering medium, one possible approach is to have a local offset between the side where the photons enter the object and where they leave it. The possible depth resolution is dependent on this offset. The theoretical resolution can be estimated by solving the optical diffusion equation or by using Monte Carlo simulations of light transport.

Fig. 2 depicts simulation results for two different local offsets in remission geometry according to the photon diffusion model.

Photon bananas (i.e., banana formed curves in the diagram) are colored depending on the probability of photons passing this area.

The spread of the photon banana characterizes which optical differences inside the tissue can be detected through this measurement.

Additionally, Fig. 2 shows that under the assumed conditions, a depth resolution of about 1cm is to be expected [23].

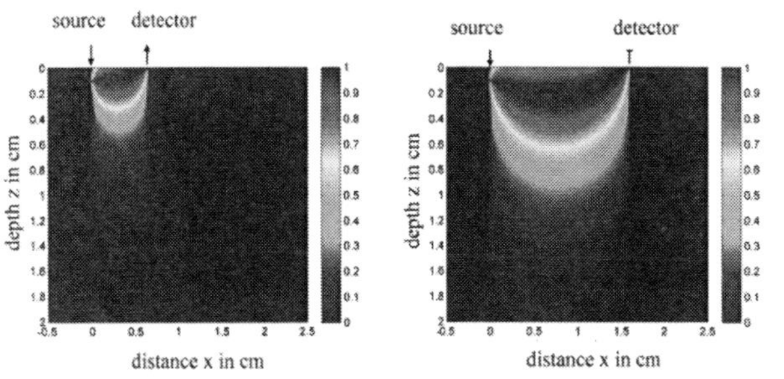

Figure 2. Photon "bananas" for two different offsets between source and detector position

B. *Experimental Realization*

1) *Experimental Setup*

Experiments were carried out with a remission geometry setup as depicted in Fig. 3 and Fig. 4. A camera is mounted perpendicular to the test object, which allows spatially-resolved detection of the diffusely reflected light.

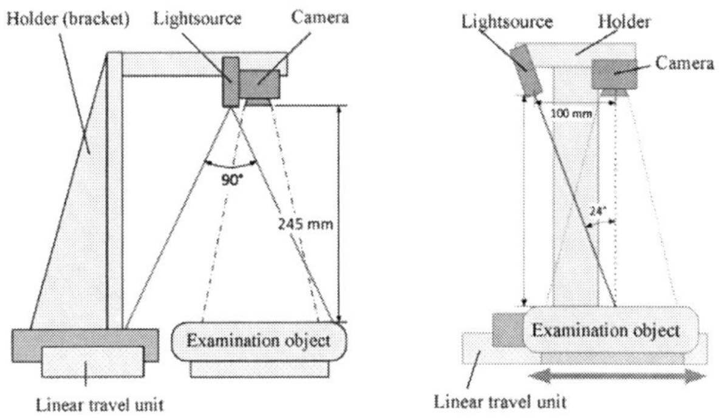

Figure 3. Scheme of the experimental setup

The line generator emits light with an angle of 24° with respect to the optical axis of the camera.

Light source and camera are mounted on a motorized translation stage and moved together over the examination object in a linear fashion.

Camera images were acquired with a step size of 1.25 mm using an exposure times of typically 4 ms to 10 ms.

A photographic image of the realized experimental setup is shown in Fig. 4. An industrial charge-coupled device (CCD) camera (Allied Vision Gruppy Pro F125) with enhanced NIR sensitivity and equipped with a high aperture c-mount objective [24] is employed as photon detector. The camera has a quantum efficiency of 24% in the wavelength range of 780-785nm, which was used for the experiments. Furthermore, the camera has a resolution of 1292x964 pixels.

The following light sources were investigated as possible line generators:

- a 785 nm high coherent continuous wave laser (cw-laser; Z-Laser Optoelektronik GmbH (DE): ZM18RF379 Z80M18S-F785-lg90),
- a 780 nm picosecond-pulsed laser (PsP; PicoQuant GmbH (DE): PDL 808 Sepia. + LDH-8-1-1097),
- a fiber coupled 780 nm incoherent high-power light emission diode (fiber-coupled LED; Thorlabs Inc. (US): M780F2).

To generate the line profile, each source was equipped with a broadband anti-reflection coated cylindrical lens.

Figure 4. Photographic image of the experimental setup

2) *Examination Object*

We used an established phantom of the female breast provided by the Physikalisch-Technische Bundesanstalt Berlin (PTB the National Metrology Institute of Germany) as examination object (Fig. 5).

The phantom has two embedded spherical lesions with a diameter of 10 mm each (Fig. 5).

The center of the superficial lesion (lesion 1) is 10mm below the surface. The center of the second lesion (lesion 2) is 25 mm below the surface. Accordingly, the top of the lesions is 5 mm respectively 20 mm below the surface.

a) Photographic image

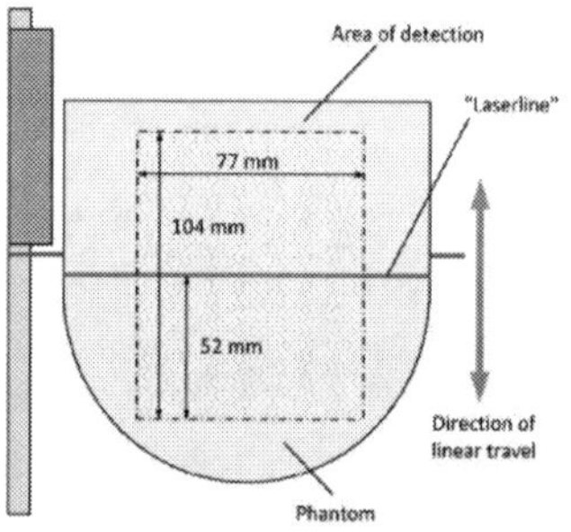

(b) Area of detection

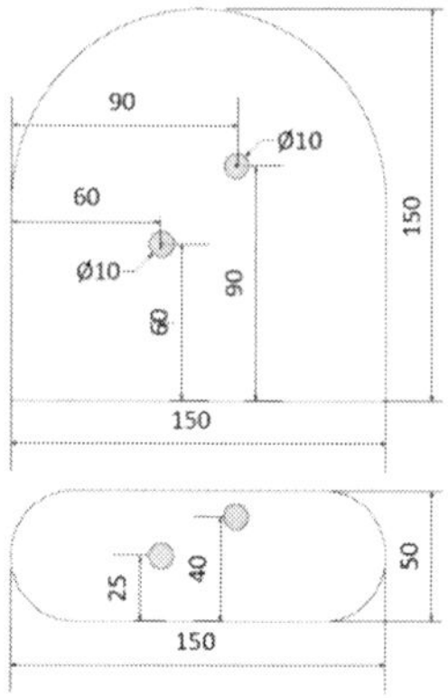

(c) Dimensions
- Top view
- Side view

Figure 5. Solid-body-phantom of the female breast.

The optical properties of the phantom are:

- μ_a(lesion 1) = 0.17 cm^{-1},
- μ_a(lesion 2) = 0.20 cm^{-1},
- μ_s'(lesion 1) = 7.9 cm^{-1},
- μ_s'(lesion 2) = 7.7 cm^{-1},
- μ_a(background) = 0.043 cm^{-1},
- μ_s'(background) = 8.3 cm^{-1}.

Both lesions exhibit roughly a 5-fold absorption-enrichment compared to the surrounding background.

III. Results and Discussion

Fig. 6 depicts the normalized absorption images of a rectangular image section (Fig. 5b) of the phantom obtained with the different light sources (see 2.2.1). The superficial lesion is detectable with all three light sources; moreover its size can be estimated to a high degree.

In contrast to lesion 1, lesion 2 that is 25 mm below the surface cannot be seen in Fig. 7. Lesion 2 remains also hidden for higher offset values due to the limits in the dynamic range and in the signal-to-noise ratio.

From these result, we conclude, that the proposed procedure:

- Is suitable to detect inhomogeneities (e.g.,, lesions) in human tissue up to a depth of 1cm,
- is most likely not adequate to find inhomogeneities (e.g., lesions) in human tissue, which are deeper than 2cm under the surface of the skin.

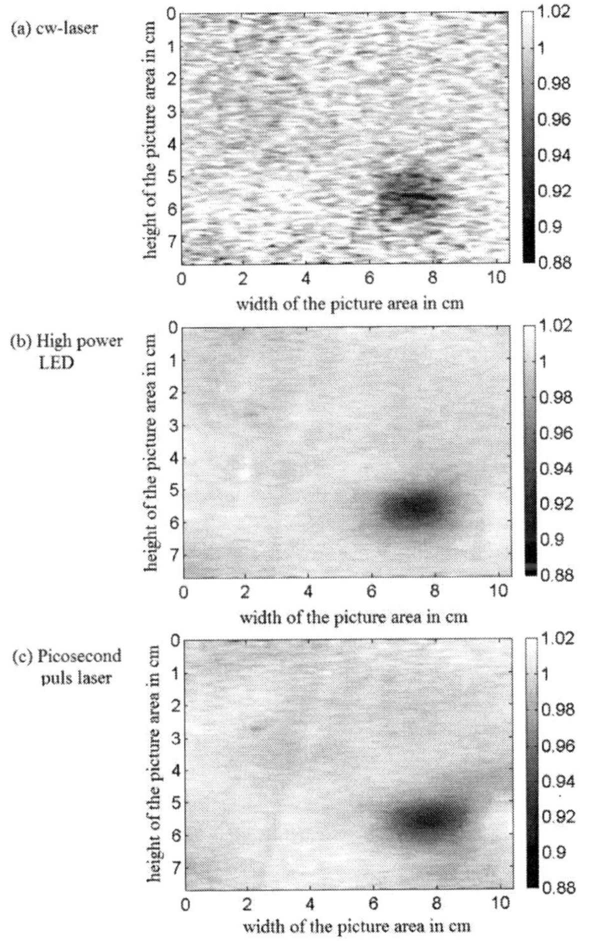

Figure 6. Detection of the lesion 1 in the phantom of a mammary

The objects in Fig. 6 show an oval-shaped distortion along the (horizontal) scan direction. As illustrated in Fig. 7, this effect is caused by the specific source-detector arrangement in our measurement. When moving source and detector with the fixed offset across a lesion, the propagation of photons is affected by the lesion two times, once for the light source and once for the detector being close to the lesion position (Fig. 7).

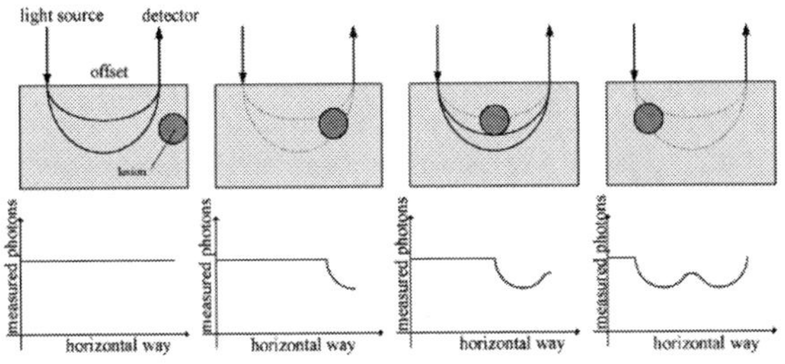

Figure 7. Horizontal distorsion

The image quality obtained with the continuous-wave laser (cw-laser) source (Fig. 6a) is worse than with the other two light sources due to the speckle effect. When using the LED light source, this effect is not present due to the incoherent nature of its light. The speckle effect is also suppressed when applying the picosecond pulsed diode laser which has a much broader spectral width than the cw-laser.

The results of the high-power LED and the picosecond-pulse-laser are similar in overall quality. Since the picosecond-pulse-laser is more expensive and more complicated in usage, we conclude that the high-power LED is the best tested light source for practical application.

This perception is confirmed by calculation of the image contrast to noise ratio (CNR) for different experiments (Tables 1, 2).

The contrast is defined as the difference in signal intensity or gray-scale value between the side of the lesion and the side of ambient tissue. Dividing this value by the ambient noise (standard deviation, SD), the result is the contrast-to-noise ratio CNR. The used region of interests (ROI) to find the signal intensity S_A of the ambient tissue, the signal intensity S_L of the detected lesion and a range to calculate the standard deviation (SD, sigma) in this study are shown in Fig. 8.

The CNR is determined over the equation:

$$CNR = \frac{|S_L - S_A|}{SD} \quad . \qquad (1)$$

S_L is the signal value at the center position of the detected lesion, while S_A is an average value and SD is the corresponding standard deviation of an ambient tissue are of 100 * 100 pixels (≈ 8 mm * 8 mm).

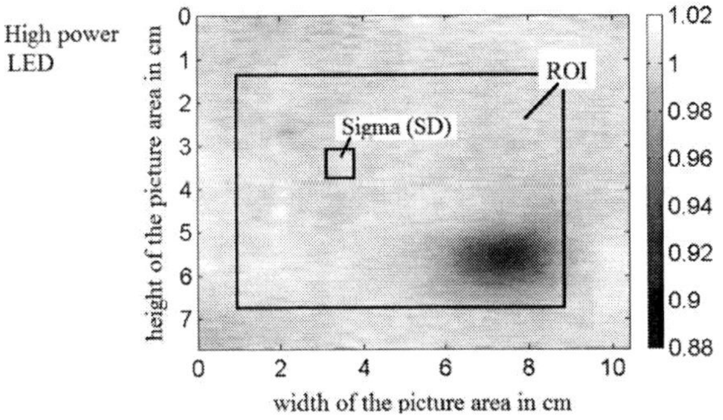

Figure 8. Special areas in the tomographic picture to calculate the contrast to noise ratio

The contrast to noise ratio in Fig. 6a (CNR = 14) is significantly worse rated than in Fig. 6b (CNR = 27) or Fig. 6c (CNR = 25).

Beside the kind of light source, other parameters have an effect to the CNR (Tables 1, 2):

- the applied power of the light source,
- the integration-time of the camera.

TABLE 1. COMPARISON OF CONTRAST TO NOISE RATIO VALUES BY USING THE LIGHT SOURCES IN A LOW INTENSITY MODE

Time of integration of the camera	CNR cw-laser	CNR Hight-power LED	CNR Picosecond pulse laser
4 ms	13	16	16
7 ms	16	22	23
10 ms	14	27	25

The general expectation is that both, an increase of the source power and an increase of the integration time of the detector, improve the CNR. But due to the speckle-effects the cw-laser produces better results in low intensity mode because the device goes below the laser threshold and acts mainly as an incoherent LED.

TABLE 2. COMPARISON OF CONTRAST TO NOISE RATIO VALUES BY USING THE LIGHT SOURCES IN A HIGH INTENSITY MODE

Time of integration of the camera	CNR cw-laser	CNR Hight-power LED	CNR Picosecond pulse laser
4 ms	10	26	26
7 ms	8	28	31
10 ms	10	33	33

With spatial averaging an additional improvement with respect to speckle-interferences can be achieved. (CNR = 64, Fig. 9).

This shows that even a coherent light source can produce a good contrast to noise ratio, if the speckle interference is eliminated. But even a CNR of 64 generated only limited additional value, i.e., the deeper positioned lesion 2 is still not detectable. Nonetheless with a higher CNR the edges of lesion 1 are less blurred.

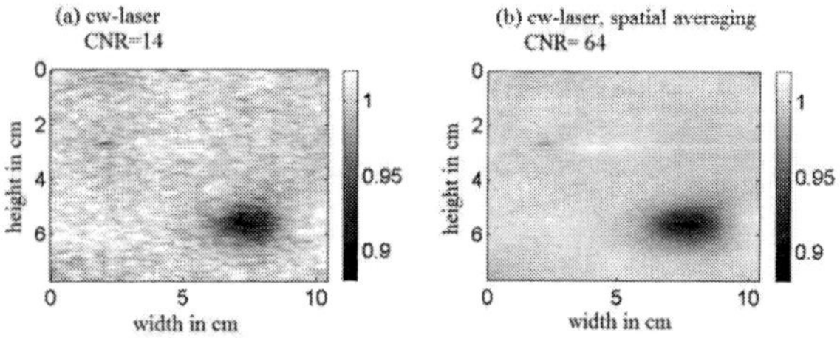

Figure 9. Comparisation of cw-laser results (a) with speckle-effect, (b) with reduced speckle-interferences by spatial averaging

The chemical and optical properties of the breast phantom are stable over long periods of time. This allowed us to conduct multiple experiments with different light sources.

Due to the similar results of the high-power LED and the picosecond-pulsed laser, the high-power LED is able to replace the more costly picosecond-pulse-laser in future tests.

Furthermore, our study shows that industrial CCD cameras are suitable detectors.

IV. CONCLUSION

In conclusion, this paper demonstrates that the proposed approach with lineshape light source and camera based detection of diffusely remitted light is feasible. With the current results we can infer that a purely optical recognition of intrinsic absorbing lesions in human tissue will be restricted to a near surface area, if our approach is used. But the actual limits of this approach have yet to be determined. For example, an increase in the local offset will likely increase the possible detection depth. To the best of our knowledge, a recognition depth of 1.5-2 cm seems practical in an assembly of remission.

Future research on the depth resolution of intrinsic absorbers in human tissue can build on the results of this study. One possibility would be the use of established liquid phantoms, which allow adjusting the depth of the lesion continuously. Since high-power LEDs are a cheap and an effective light source for this kind of experiments, we hope that this will enable more research in this area.

Due to the fact that the lesions in the used phantom are considered being realistic models of typical pathological changes in human tissue, the results for in-vivo investigations are expected to be similar.

With this in mind, the results seem to be very promising, since the proposed method has a high potential for medical diagnostic procedures.

REFERENCES

[1] A. P. Gibson, J .C. Hebden, and S. R. Arridge, "Recent advancesin diffuse optical imaging", Phys. Med. Biol., vol. 50, 2005, pp.1–43, Feb. 2005, doi:10.1088/0031-9155/50/4/R01.

[2] D. Grosenick, H. Rinneberg, R. Cubeddu, and P. Taroni, "Review of optical breast imaging and spectroscopy.," J. Biomed. Opt., vol. 21(9), pp. 091311_1-27, Jul. 2016, doi:10.1117/1.JBO.21.9.091311.

[3] A. N. Sen, S. P. Gopinath, and C. S. Robertson, "Clinical application of near-infrared spectroscopy in patients with traumatic brain injury: a review of the progress of the field.," Neurophotonics, vol. 3(3), pp. 031409_1-5, Jul. 2016, doi:10.1117/1.NPh.3.3.031409.

[4] G. Greisen, B. Andresen, A. M. Plomgaard, and S. Hyttel-Sørensen, "Cerebral oximetry in preterm infants: an agenda for research with a clear clinical goal.," Neurophotonics, vol. 3(3), pp. 031407_1-7, Jul. 2016, doi:10.1117/1.NPh.3.3.031407.

[5] F. Moreau, R. Yang, V. Nambiar, A. M. Demchuk, and J. F. Dunn, "Near-infrared measurements of brain oxygenation in stroke.," Neurophotonics, vol. 3(3), pp. 031403_1-8, Jul. 2016, doi:10.1117/1.NPh.3.3.031403.

[6] B. Grassi and V. Quaresima, "Near-infrared spectroscopy and skeletal muscle oxidative function in vivo in health and disease: a review from an exercise physiology perspective.," J. Biomed. Opt., vol. 21(9), pp. 091313 1-20, Sep. 2016, doi: 10.1117/1.JBO.21.9.091313.

[7] G. Hu, Q. Zhang, V. Ivkovic, and G. E. Strangman, "Ambulatory diffuse optical tomography and multimodality physiological monitoring system for muscle and exercise applications.," J. Biomed. Opt., vol. 21(9), pp. 91314ff, Sep. 2016, doi:10.1117/1.JBO.21.9.091314.

[8] B. Ebert, J. Voigt, R. Macdonald, U. Schneider, A. Thomas, B. Hamm, and K.-G. A. Hermann, "Detection of rheumatoid arthritis using non-specific contrast enhanced fluorescence imaging", Acad. Radiol., vol. 17(3), pp. 375–381, Mar. 2010, doi: 10.1016/j.acra.2009.09.016. Epub 2009 Dec 6.

[9] X. Intes, J. Ripoll, Y. Chen, S. Nioka, A. G. Yodh, and B. Chance, "In vivo continuouswave optical breast imaging enhanced with indocyanine green," Med Phys., vol.30(6), pp. 1039-1047, Jun. 2003, doi: 10.1118/1.1573791.

[10] B. Alacam, B. Yazici, X. Intes, and B. Chance, "Analysis of ICG pharmacokinetics in cancerous tumors using NIR optical methods." Conf Proc IEEE Eng Med Biol Soc., 2005, pp. 62-65, doi: 10.1109/IEMBS.2005.1616342.

[11] B. Alacam, B. Yazici, X. Intes, S. Nioka, and B. Chance, "Pharmacokinetic-rate images of indocyanine green for breast tumors using near-infrared optical methods," Phys. Med. Biol., vol. 53, pp. 837–859, Jan. 2008, doi:10.1088/0031-9155/53/4/002.

[12] Y. Tsujino, K. Mizumoto, Y. Matsuzaka, H. Niihara, and E. Morita, "Fluorescence navigation with indocyanine green for detecting sentinel nodes in extramammary Paget's disease and squamous cell carcinoma." J Dermatol., vol. 36(2), pp. 90- 94, Feb. 2009, doi: 10.1111/j.1346-8138.2009.00595.x

[13] A. Hagen, D. Grosenick, R. Macdonald, H. Rinneberg, S. Burock, P. Warnick, A. Poellinger, and P. M. Schlag, "Late-fluorescence mammography assesses tumor capillary permeability and differentiates malignant from benign lesions," Opt Express., vol. 17(19), pp. 17016-17033, Sep. 2009, doi: 10.1364/OE.17.017016

[14] A. Poellinger, S. Burock, D. Grosenick, A. Hagen, L. Lüdemann, F. Diekmann, F. Engelken, R. Macdonald, H. Rinneberg, and P. M. Schlag, "Breast cancer: early- and latefluorescence near-infrared imaging with indocyanine green--a preliminary study," Radiology, vol. 258(2), pp. 409-416, Feb. 2011, doi: 10.1148/radiol.10100258.

[15] S. G. Werner, H. Langer, P. Schott, M. Bahner, M. Schwenke, G. Lind-Albrecht, F. Spiecker, B. Kurtz, G. R. Burmester, and M. Backhaus, "Indocyanine green-enhanced fluorescence optical imaging in patients with early and very early arthritis: a comparative study with magnetic resonance imaging." Arthritis Rheum., vol. 65(12), pp. 3036 – 3044, Dec.2013, doi: 10.1002/art.38175.

[16] V. Ntziachristos and B. Chance, "Probing physiology and molecular function using optical imaging: applications to breast cancer." Breast Cancer Res., vol. 3(1), pp. 41-46, 2001, doi:10.1186/bcr269.

[17] V. Ntziachristos, A. G. Yodh, M. Schnall, and B. Chance, "Concurrent MRI and diffuse optical tomography of breast after indocyanine green enhancement." Proc Natl Acad Sci USA., vol. 97(6), pp. 2767-2772, Mar 2000, doi: 10.1073/pnas.040570597.

[18] B. Zhu and E. M. Sevick-Muraca, "A review of performance of near-infrared fluorescence imaging devices used in clinical studies," The British Journal of Radiology, vol. 88(1045), pp. 1-26, Dec. 2014, doi: 10.1259/bjr.20140547

[19] A. Corlu, R. Choe, T. Durduran, M. A. Rosen, M. Schweiger, S. R. Arridge, M. D. Schnall, and A. G. Yodh, "Three-dimensional in vivo fluorescence diffuse optical tomography of breast cancer in humans," Opt Express., vol. 15(11), pp. 6696-6716, May 2007, doi: 10.1364/OE.15.006696.

[20] D. Grosenick, H. Wabnitz, and B. Ebert, "Review: Recent advances in contrast-enhanced near infrared diffuse optical imaging of diseases using indocyanine green," J. Near Infrared Spectrosc., vol. 20(1), pp. 203–221, Dec. 2011, doi: 10.1255/jnirs.964

[21] T. J. Muldoon, S. A. Burgess, B. R. Chen, D. Ratner, and E. M. C. Hillman, "Analysis of skin lesions using laminar optical tomography". Biomed. Opt. Express., vol. 3(7), pp. 1701-1712, Jun 2012, doi: 10.1364/BOE.3.001701.

[22] S. A. Burgess, D. Ratner, B. R. Chen, and E. M. C. Hillman, "Fiber-optic and articulating arm implementations of laminar optical tomography for clinical applications." Biomed. Opt. Express., vol. 1(3), pp. 780-790, Sep. 2010, doi: 10.1364/BOE.1.000780

[23] R. Freyer, "Development of an optical image giving procedure for the medical diagnostics,", („Entwicklung eines optischen Bildgebungsverfahrens zur medizinischen Diagnostik.") , master thesis HTW Berlin, May 2015, unpublished

[24] A. Hagen, "Method and device for aquiring optical depth information of an optical scattering object", DE patent DE102015107485B3, (WO002016180404A1), 29. Sep. 2016

[25] A. Bailleu, A. Hagen, D. Hofmann, "Format-filling digitization of handlarge parts of the body and 3D-Rekonstruktion of the objects for favorable medical application," („Formatfüllende Digitalisierung handgroßer Körperteile und 3D-Rekonstruktion der Objekte zur vorteilhaften medizinischen Anwendung.") In:. Digitalisierung: Menschen zählen. Beiträge und Positionen der HTW Berlin, Hg. Matthias Knaut, BWV Berliner Wissenschafts-Verlag, vol. 6, pp. 252-257, Nov. 2016, ISBN 978-3-8305-3700-7

[26] A. Bailleu, A. Hagen, „3D-Rekonstruktion of handlarge parts of the body with diagnostically relevant depth information in the surface texture,", („3D-Rekonstruktion handgroßer Körperteile mit diagnostisch relevanten Tiefeninformationen in der Oberflächentextur." In: 3D-Nordost, GfAI, pp. 133-142, Dec.2016, ISBN 978-3-942709-16-3

[27] P. Azad, T. Gockel, R. Dillmann, "Computer Vision–Principles and Practice," Elektor International Media, 2008, ISBN: 978-0905705712 (German: 2007, ISBN: 978-3895761652).

Effects of the WSN Deployment Environment on MaxMin and LQI-DCP Multihop Clustering Protocols

Chérif Diallo

Laboratoire Algébre, Cryptographie, Codes et Applications (ACCA)
UFR Sciences appliquées et de Technologies (UFR SAT)
Université Gaston Berger, BP 234 Saint-Louis, Sénégal
Email: cherif.diallo@ugb.edu.sn

***Abstract*—In wireless networking, clustering techniques add scalability, reduce the computation complexity of routing protocols, allow data aggregation and then enhance the network performance. The well known MaxMin clustering algorithm was previously generalized, corrected and validated. In [1] we improve MaxMin by proposing a Single-node Cluster Reduction (SNCR) mechanism which eliminates single-node clusters and then improve energy efficiency. In this paper, we show that MaxMin, because of its original pathological case, does not support the grid deployment topology, which is frequently used in WSN architectures. The unreliability feature of the wireless links could have negative impacts on Link Quality Indicator (LQI) based clustering protocols. So, in the second part of this paper we show how our distributed Link Quality based d-Clustering Protocol (LQI-DCP) has good performance in high unreliable link environments. Performance evaluation results also show that LQI-DCP fully supports the grid deployment topology.**

Keywords–Wireless Sensor Network; Multihop Clustering; LQI; MaxMin; LQI-DCP.

I. Introduction and Backgrounds

In a cold chain monitoring application, due to the size of a warehouse which hosts large numbers of pallets, provided each with a temperature sensor, the Wireless Sensor Network (WSN) can reach several hundreds of nodes which collaborate for sending alarms towards the Base Station (BS). This application specifically collects rare events (alarms) to ensure the proper monitoring of the system. If the temperature is over a threshold, an alarm will be generated; this "interesting event" is then sent towards the BS. In such a context, network clustering techniques add scalability feature and then reduce the computation complexity of data gathering and routing protocols.

The more often WSN architecture used in cold chain monitoring applications is the grid deployment topology. So, in this paper, we show that one should be careful with the MaxMin clustering heuristic [2] in such a topology.

In [1] and [3], we show how it is important to sufficiently outspread clusterhead in oder to reduce cluster overlaps, the amount of channel contention between clusters and energy wastefulness due to overhearing phenomenon. The MaxMin clustering heuristic, as proposed in [2][4], has the drawback of not taking into account this problem. In order to solve this issue, we have proposed LQI-DCP in [5]. LQI-DCP is an energy efficient LQI based protocol which aims to construct multihop clusters by producing clusters of which each clusterhead has a better positioning regarding the locations of other clusterheads. The clusterheads resulting from LQI-DCP are sufficiently outspread. LQI-DCP also reduces the density of clusterheads and then improves the WSN energy efficiency, while each sensor still remains at most d-hops away from its own clusterhead.

In a cold chain monitoring application, the warehouse hosts hundreds of pallets, one upon the other. This environment is subjected to some unreliability of the wireless links. So, it is important for LQI based clustering schemes to fully support such an environment. This is the main objective of the second part of this paper.

Previous works [1][2][4] present details on MaxMin, whereas LQI-DCP is described in [5]. All clusterhead selection criteria used in this paper are defined in [1][5]. As in [1][5] we indifferently use caryomme(s) or clusterhead(s).

To carry out our work, this paper is organized as follows: the MaxMin Pathological Case is described in tne next section. Consequently, we explain, in the third section, why MaxMin does not support the grid deployment topology. Then, in the fourth section, we present how LQI-DCP is well adapted for the grid deployment topology. Finally, the last two parts present performance results pertaining to the LQI-DCP protocol when one takes into account the unreliability feature of the wireless links.

II. The MaxMin Pathological Case

Given the similarities with Linked Cluster Algorithm (LCA) [6] and LCA2 [7], MaxMin naturally inherits the same pathological case. Thus, in the original paper [4] which revealed MaxMin to the scientific research community, the authors reported the pathological case for which MaxMin fails in the process of cluster formation. We reproduce here the figure (see Figure 1) and the argument as they were stated in [4] : *"There is a known configuration where the proposed heuristic fails to provide a good solution. This configuration is when node ids are monotonically increasing or decreasing in a straight line. In this case, the* $d+1$ *smallest node ids belong to the same cluster as shown in Figure 1. All other nodes become clusterheads of themselves only. Again, while this is not optimal it still guarantees that no node is more than d-hops away from a clusterhead. Furthermore, this configuration is highly unlikely in a real world application. However, this is a topic of future work to be performed with this heuristic."*

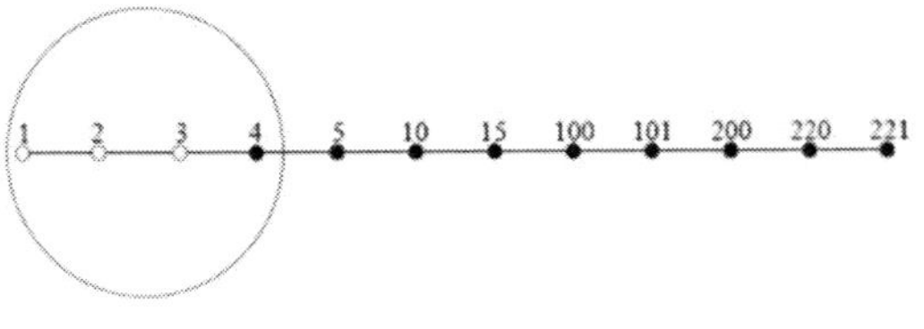

Figure 1. Worse case performance scenario for MaxMin [4]

In the next section, we will show how this pathological case has negative impacts on the grid deployment topology. Indeed, the authors of [4] said that : "*Furthermore, this configuration is highly unlikely in a real world application*". This is obviously wrong because the grid deployment topology is more often encountered in real WSN applications, especially in a cold chain monitoring application.

III. MaxMin incompatibility with the grid deployment topology

To better understand the consequences of the MaxMin pathological case on the grid deployment topology, let us consider the representation in Figure 2 where N nodes are deployed on a rectangular area of length L and width l. Considering a grid where each side of the area is subdivided with a constant pitch λ. Then, the coordinates $x(i)$ and $y(i)$ of the ith node $i \in [\![1, N]\!]$ are obtained as follows:
$n = \lfloor \frac{L}{\lambda} \rfloor$, $m = \lfloor \frac{l}{\lambda} \rfloor$, $N = ((n+1)*(m+1)) - 1$, where $\lfloor \frac{L}{\lambda} \rfloor$ denotes the integer part of $\frac{L}{\lambda}$
$x(i) = \lambda * \lfloor \frac{i}{m+1} \rfloor$
$y(i) = \lambda * i \bmod (n+1)$

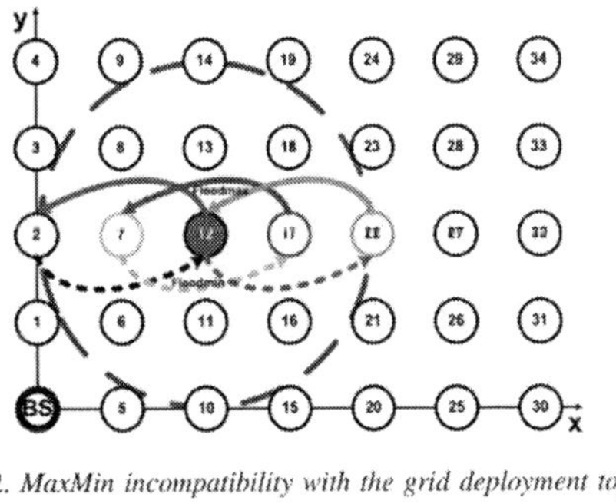

Figure 2. *MaxMin incompatibility with the grid deployment topology*

If we assume that all nodes have the same transmission range $R = 2 * \lambda$, then by running MaxMin algorithm with the parameter $d = 1$ and the function criteria $f(x) = id(x)$ for the WSN example in (Figure 2):

- During **floodmax** phase, the node 2 receives the value 12 from 12th node.
- Next, the node 12 receives this value 12 from 2th node during the **floodmin** phase.
- Accordingly, the 12th node is selected as clusterhead.
- As far as that goes, all the ith nodes, $i \in [\![10, 30]\!]$ (Figure 2), are selected as clusterhead.
- More generally, it's easy to show that all the ith nodes $i \in [\![2(m+1), N]\!]$ are selected as clusterhead by MaxMin.

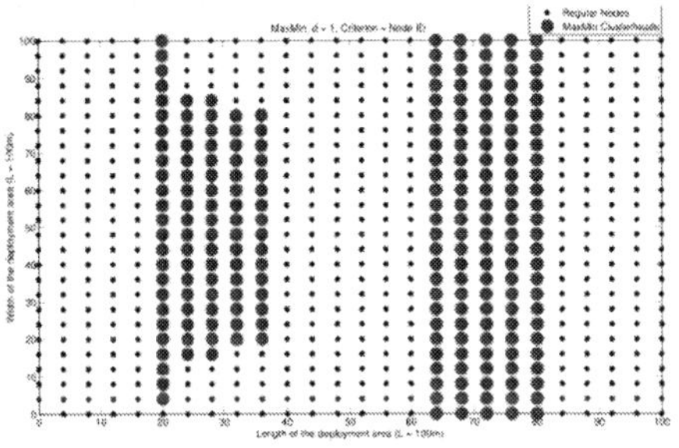

Figure 3. MaxMin: Average clusterhead locations, Node ID criterion, $d = 1$

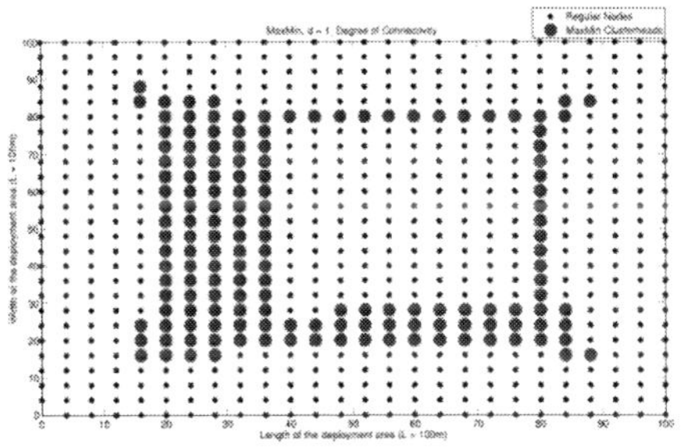

Figure 4. MaxMin: Average clusterhead locations, Degree of Connectivity criterion, $d = 1$

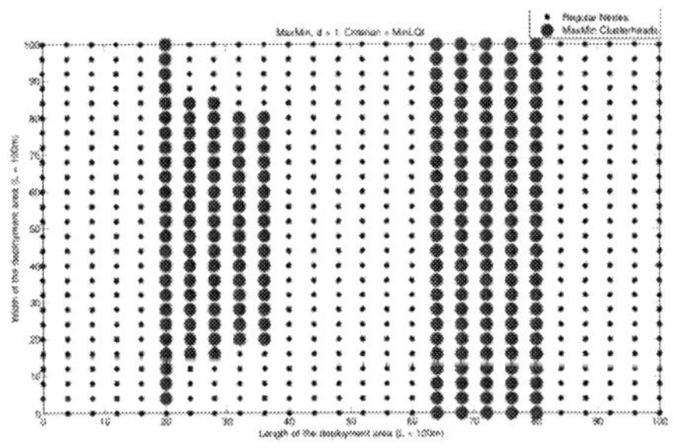

Figure 5. MaxMin: Average clusterhead locations, MinLQI criterion, $d = 1$

Thus, it is important to be careful when one chooses the criteria used to select the MaxMin clusterheads in the context of a grid deployment topology. Indeed, the "degree of connectivity" and "MinLQI" criteria also suffer the same effects because of the smoothness of the grid topology. These critera are monotonically increasing in each row and each column of the grid when one moves from the edge toward the center of the deployment area.

Thus, MaxMin run with the Single-Node cluster reduction mechanism (SNCR) [1] leads to the following results for criteria: "Node id" (Figure 3), "Degree of connectivity" (Figure 4), and "MinLQI" (Figure 5). These results are explained by the neighbourhood relationship (transmission range) between the selected clusterheads. So, we obtain a series of clusterheads located in adjacent columns which are periodically seperated by adjacent columns composed of regular nodes (Figure 5).

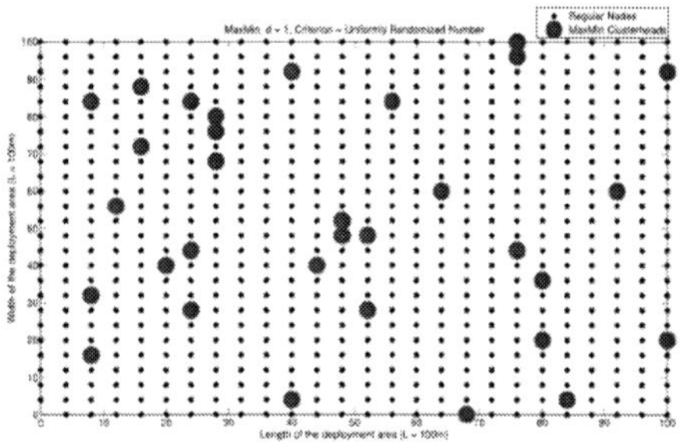

Figure 6. MaxMin: Average clusterhead locations, Randomized Criterion, $d = 1$

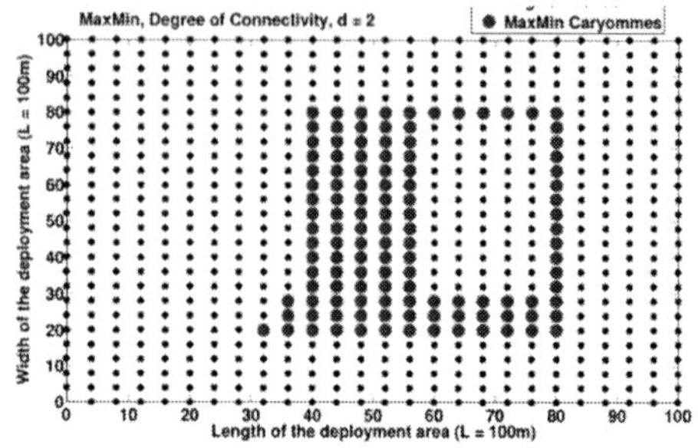

Figure 7. *MaxMin: Average clusterhead locations, degree of connectivity criterion,* $d = 2$

To overcome this issue of MaxMin pathological case in a grid deployment topology, one should choose a criterion function of which the values are randomly distributed to the nodes. This helps avoiding a function which is monotonically increasing (or decreasing) along the lines of the grid. This randomization of the criterion overcomes the problem of MaxMin pathological case (Figure 6) but also has the disadvantage of leading to unpredictable results. Indeed, the benefits of choosing a particular criterion rather than another one is to promote optimal results with respect to the main objectives of the application according to its operational conditions. Figure 6 shows the location of caryommes obtained for a randomized function criteria. As we can see, this result is not optimal because some clusterheads are too closely located. Therefore, this leads to high energy consumption because of overhearing, channel contention and overlaps between clusters [1].

According to these results, we tend to conclude that MaxMin is not suitable for the grid deployment topology which is by far the most common topology encountered in cold chain monitoring applications.

The MaxMin pathological case is also a big drawback for multihop clusters, $d \geq 2$, as shown in Figure 7.

To overcome this problem with MaxMin, as we stated in Section III, one should choose a criterion function of which the values are randomly distributed to the nodes. This helps avoiding a function which is monotonically increasing (or decreasing) along the lines of the grid. Even in this case, LQI-DCP (Figure 10) is more efficient than MaxMin (Figure 11) by sufficiently outspreading selected clusterheads.

Conversely our LQI-DCP protocol fully supports the grid deployment topology both for 1-hop and for multihop WSN clustering (Figures 8 and 9).

IV. LQI Model for Performance Evaluation Purposes

At each given time t, the LQI value of the link formed by any pair (x, y) of nodes is calculated by using the $\ell(x, y, t)$ function defined below:

$$\ell(x, y, t) = f(x, y, t) * g(x, y) \quad (1)$$

$$f(x, y, t) = 1 - Pr\left[\ell ink(x, y, t) = Unreliable\right] \quad (2)$$

$$g(x, y) = \alpha + \frac{\beta * \log(1 + (\gamma(x, y) - \gamma_{min}(x)))}{\log(1 + \gamma_{max}(x))} \quad (3)$$

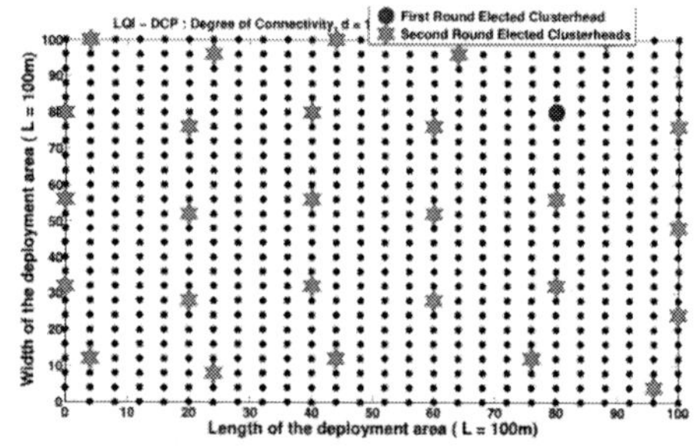

Figure 8. *LQI-DCP: Average clusterhead locations, degree of connectivity criterion,* $d = 1$

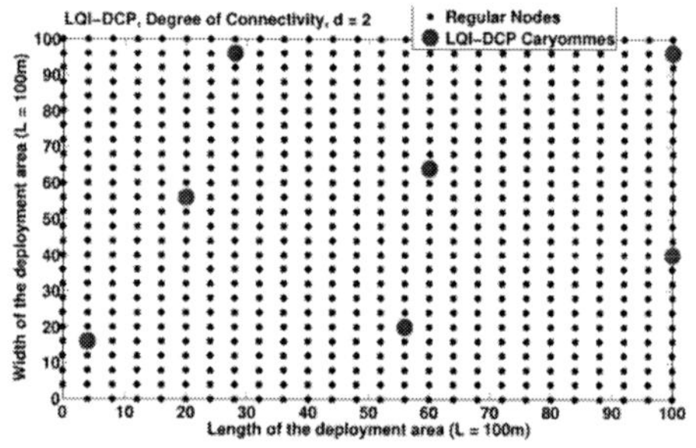

Figure 9. *LQI-DCP: Average clusterhead locations, degree of connectivity criterion,* $d = 2$

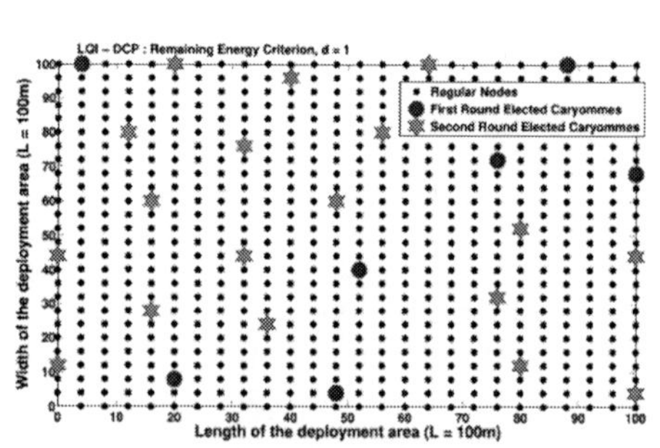

Figure 10. *LQI-DCP: Average clusterhead locations, Remaining Energy Criterion,* $d = 1$

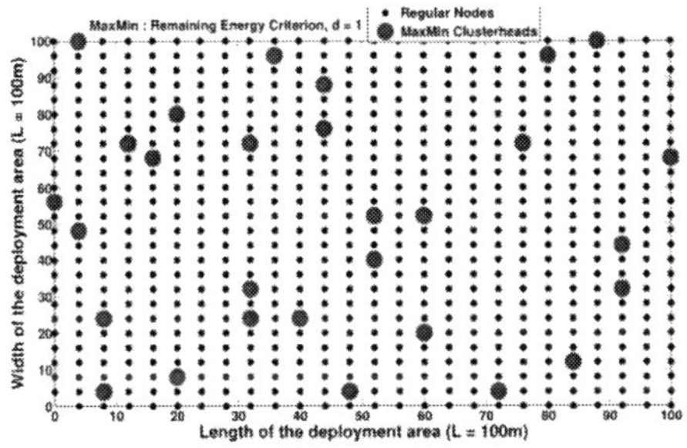

Figure 11. *MaxMin: Average clusterhead locations, Remaining Energy Criterion,* $d = 1$

$$\gamma(x, y) = \frac{1}{d(x, y)} \quad (4)$$

$$\gamma_{min}(x) = \min_{y \in \mathcal{N}_1(x)} \gamma(x, y) \quad (5)$$

$$\gamma_{max}(x) = \max_{y \in \mathcal{N}_1(x)} \gamma(x, y) \quad (6)$$

where $\alpha = 50$, $\beta = 255$ and $d(x, y)$ is the distance separating y from x.

In the context of a cold chain monitoring application, the warehouse hosts hundreds of pallets, one upon the other. Each pallets is provided with a temperature sensor. This environment is subjected to some unreliabilities of the wireless links. So, in the formula (2), $Pr[\ell ink(x, y, t) = Unreliable]$ denotes the probability that the link $\ell ink(x, y, t)$ becomes unreliable at time t. This probability is used in some simulation scenarios, in order to evaluate the behavior of our LQI-DCP protocol with respect to the unrelibility aspect of the wireless links.

The choice of this model, formula (3), is guided by experimental results shown in [8] and [9], which stated that the LQI decreases when the distance between nodes increases in Zigbee-based WSN.

As we can see, $\ell(x, y, t) \neq \ell(y, x, t)$, because of the formulas (5) and (6). Hence, the model allows to take into account asymetrical aspects of the wireless links.

For moteiv's Tmote Sky [10] sensors equipped with chipcon's CC2420 [11], the LQI values range from 50 to 110. Even so, we stick with the ZigBee standard [12],[13] because some manufacturers, such as Sun-SPOT [14] and WiEye [15], are still using the standard LQI values. Then, we use the standard values (i.e., $[0, 255]$) increased by $\alpha = 50$, instead of those of CC2420. The use of $\alpha = 50$ allows to keep the null value, $\ell(x, y, t) = 0$, only for the two cases where the node y is not in the transmission range of the node x, or when the $\ell ink(x, y, t)$ becomes unreliable i.e., $Pr[\ell ink(x, y, t) = Unreliable] = 1$.

This LQI model is only used for simulation purposes, so sensor nodes do not compute these above formulas.

Simulations, using Matlab, are run for a network size ranging from 200 to 4000 nodes. The performance results presented here are obtained by averaging the results for 100 different simulations for the two scenarios (Figures 12 and 13). As for others scenarios 80 different simulations were run. For each simulation, a new random node layout is used. In all simulation results presented below, $\ell_{max} = 230$ and $\ell_{min} = 70$ as defined in [5]. The MinLQI clusterhead selection criterion is also defined in [1]. For a node, the MinLQI value represents the minimum LQI value beyond a given threshold which is set to 100, in all simulation scenarios.

V. IMPACTS OF THE UNRELIABILITY FEATURE OF THE WIRELESS LINKS ON LQI-DCP OPERATIONS

In the context of a cold chain monitoring application, the warehouse hosts hundreds of pallets, one upon the other. Each pallets is provided with a temperature sensor. This environment is subjected to some unreliabilities of wireless links. In this section we take into account such a phenomenon. For a sensor S_i, its unreliable links with some neighbors are modeled by the Bernoulli distribution of parameter p which takes the value "unreliable" with the probability defined as follows:

$$Pr[\ell ink(i, j, t) = Unreliable] = 1 \text{ , } if \; \delta(i, j, t) \leq p \quad (7)$$

where $\delta(i, j)$ is a random generated number which is uniformly distributed in $]0, 1]$ for each neighbor S_j of the sensor S_i. If $Pr[\ell ink(i, j, t) = Unreliable] = 1$, then at time t, $\ell(i, j, t) = 0$ and the node S_j would not become a whipping boy node related to the emissary node S_i even if S_j is too closely located to S_i.

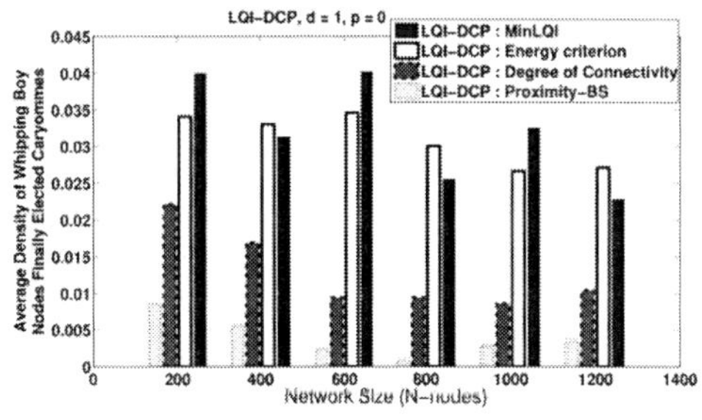

Figure 12. *LQI-DCP: Average density of whipping boy nodes finally selected as clusterheads,* $d = 1$, $p = 0$

Before inspecting the impacts of the unreliability feature of the wireless links, it is useful to examine the average ratio of the whipping boy nodes finally elected as clusterheads in the scenario where all links are considered reliable, i.e.:

$$\forall t, \; \forall x \in V, \; Pr[\ell ink(x, y, t) = Unreliable] = 0 \text{ , } \forall y \in \mathcal{N}_1(x). \quad (8)$$

Then Figure 12 plots the average number of the whipping boy nodes finally selected as clusterheads divided by the overall number of clusterheads produced by LQI-DCP. For all studied criteria, this ratio is too low. For the proximity with respect to the BS, around 1% of clusterheads are choosen from the whipping boy nodes. This ratio is between 1% and $2,5\%$ for the degree of connectivity criterion and between 3% and 4% for the MinLQI criterion.

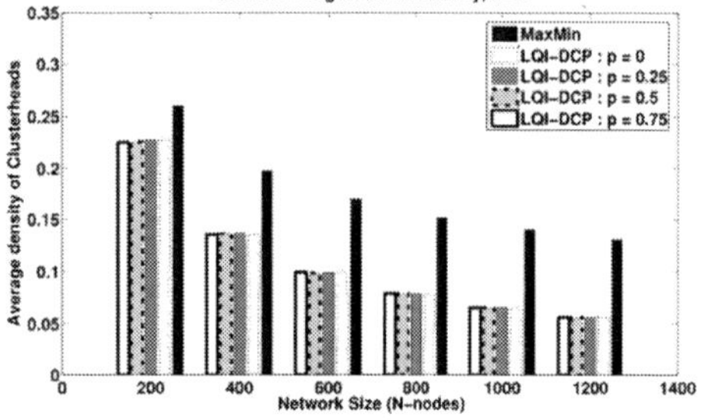

Figure 13. *LQI-DCP: Average density of clusterheads, degree of connectivity criterion,* $d = 1$

Figure 13 shows that the unreliability of the wireless links has negligible effects on the average density of clusterheads by comparing results for $p = 0$ (all links are reliable), $p = 0.25$, $p = 0.5$ and $p = 0.75$ (high unreliability), when the degree of connectivity is used as criterion. Figure 14 displays the average positions of clusterheads for $p = 0.75$. In these scenarios, no unreliability is taken into account for the MaxMin clustering scheme. Wireless link unrelibilities are only considered for the LQI-DCP clustering scheme.

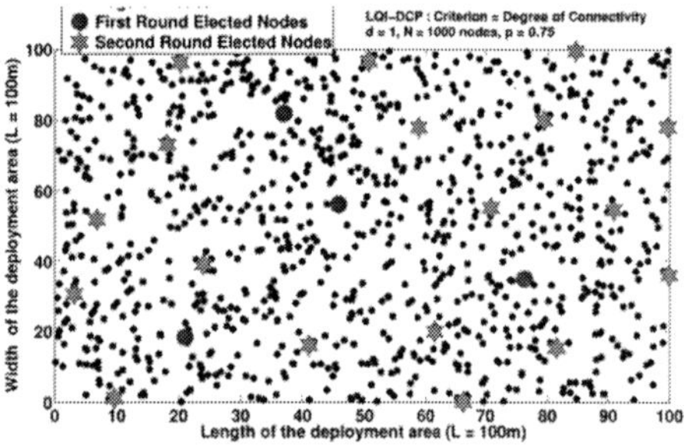

Figure 14. *LQI-DCP: Average clusterhead locations, degree of connectivity criterion,* $d = 1$, $p = 0.75$

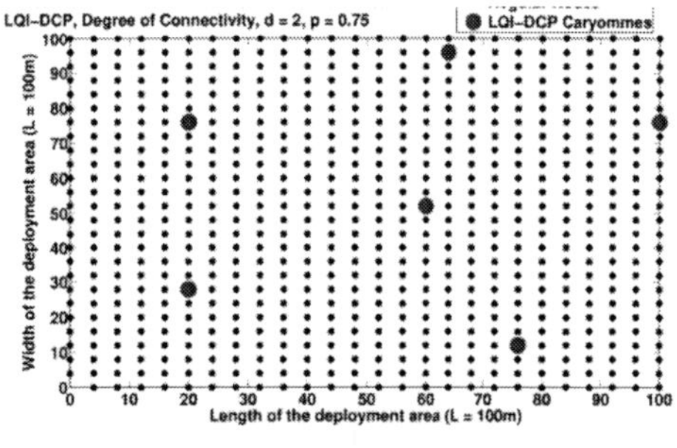

Figure 15. *LQI-DCP: Average clusterhead locations, degree of connectivity criterion,* $R = 20m$, $p = 0.75$, *multihop clusters* $d = 2$.

This result (Figure 15) is remarkable, because for $R = 20m$ and $d = 2$, it means that high unrelibilities of the wireless links ($p = 0.75$) do not have negative impacts on LQI-DCP.

For MaxMin protocol, in the results (Figures 13, 16 and 18), the unreliability feature of the wireless links is not taken

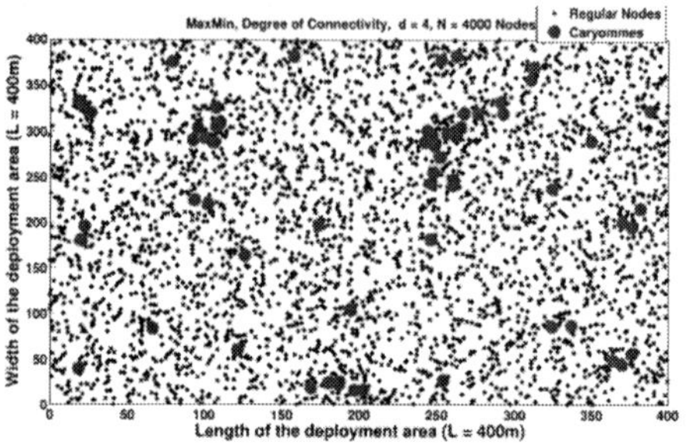

Figure 16. *MaxMin: Average clusterhead locations, degree of connectivity criterion,* N = *4000 Nodes,* $R = 20m$, $p = 0$, *multihop clusters* $d = 4$.

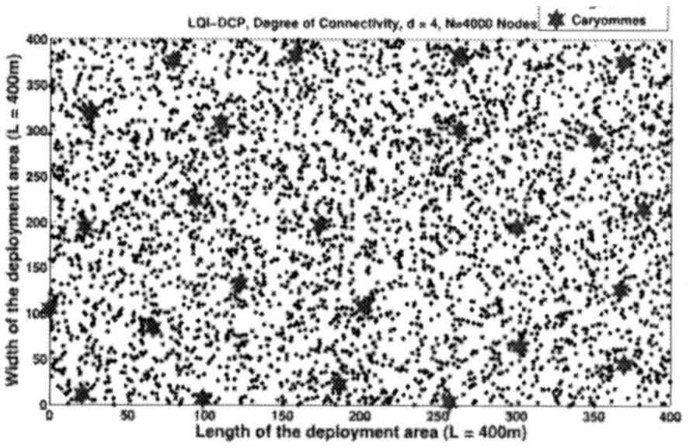

Figure 17. *LQI-DCP: Average clusterhead locations, degree of connectivity criterion,* N = *4000 Nodes,* $R = 20m$, $p = 0.75$, *multihop clusters* $d = 4$.

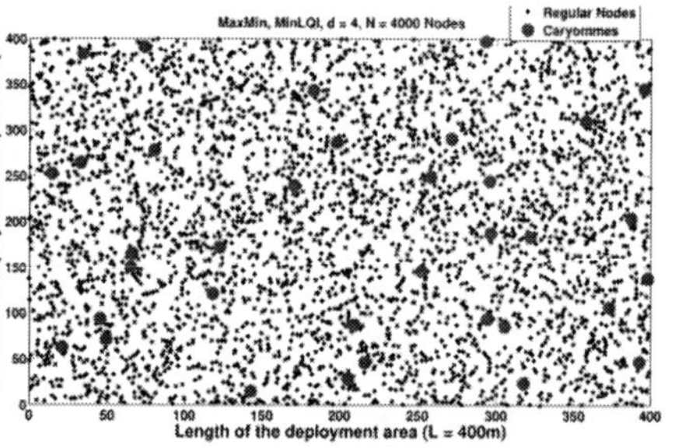

Figure 18. *MaxMin: Average clusterhead locations, MinLQI criterion,* N = *4000 Nodes,* $R = 20m$, $p = 0$, *multihop clustering* $d = 4$.

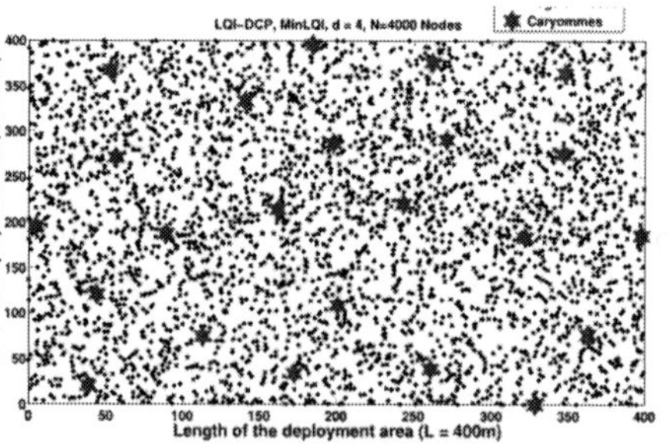

Figure 19. *LQI-DCP: Average clusterhead locations, MinLQI criterion,* N = *4000 Nodes,* $R = 20m$, $p = 0.75$, *multihop clustering* $d = 4$.

into account. Then for all scenario in this paper, $p = 0$, for MaxMin protocol. The unreliability feature of the wireless links is taken into consideration only for LQI-DCP.

Figures 14, 15, 17 and 19 plot, for LQI-DCP, the average clusterheads location when the WSN is subjected to high unreliability phenomenon of the wireless links, i.e., $p = 0.75$.

These results show that the unreliability of the wireless links also has negligible effects on the locations of clusterheads selected by LQI-DCP: caryommes are sufficiently outspread. If a link were to be unreliable, the only effect on LQI-DCP is to decrease the number of whipping boy nodes in both first and second round of the LQI-DCP process. As a neighbor of a first round elected node can not become a clusterhead. Then unreliability of the wireless links has low impact on the LQI-DCP clustering scheme.

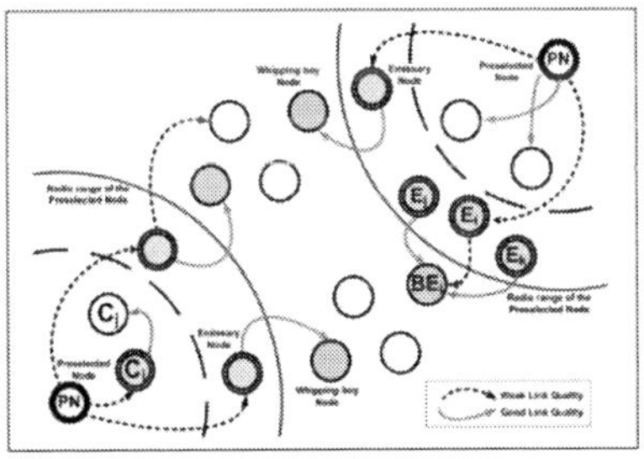

Figure 20. *Stability of LQI-DCP in unreliable link environments*

For explanation, consider the example illustrated in Figure 20, in which we suppose that the sensor C_i, although located closely to the preselected node PN, also forms a link of poor quality with PN, i.e., $\ell(PN, C_i) \leq \ell_{min}$. Thus C_i would be an "emissary node" of PN. However, even if C_i has a good link quality with C_j, i.e., $\ell(C_i, C_j) \geq \ell_{max}$, C_j will not become a "whipping boy node", relatively to C_i, because it is already clusterized and attached to PN as clusterhead [5].

In the same example (Figure 20), the unreliability of the wireless links could also affect the quality of the link formed by the emissary node E_i with the sensor BE_i. Which might result in considering BE_i as a non-clusterized regular node which is not a "whipping boy node". However, in a dense WSN, BE_i could have some good links with other emissaries such as E_j or E_k. In this case, BE_i would become a "whipping boy node" (Figure 20). This property could be less true in cases where the WSN is deployed with a low node density.

So, as we can see, in dense wireless sensor networks, our LQI-DCP protocol also supports the unreliability feature of the wireless links.

VI. Conclusion and Future Work

This paper complements our previous contributions [1] and [5]. Firstly, it shows how MaxMin is not fully compatible with the prevalent grid deployment topology. So, because of the smoothness of this topology, MaxMin fails with most of the criteria used in clusterhead selection such as "Degree of connectivity", "node id", "MinLQI", and "Proximity-BS". Then, the only way to use MaxMin in a grid deployment topology is to choose a radomized criterion function. However, in doing so, it becomes impossible to choose the most appropriate criteria for a specific application.

Secondly, we complete the LQI-DCP contribution with some results which show that this protocol fully supports the grid deployment topology. LQI-DCP is also performant in environments subjected to high unreliabilities of the wireless links. This property is important for a LQI based multihop clustering protocol such LQI-DCP.

Finally, it can be noted that the issue of security has not been addressed here. Thus, in our future work, we will be interested in the aspects of securing the LQI-DCP protocol while taking care to minimize energy consumption.

Acknowledgment

The author would like to thank "Centre d'Excellence en Mathématiques, Informatique et TIC (CEA-MITIC)" ; UFR Sciences appliquées et de Technologies (UFR SAT), Université Gaston Berger, Saint-Louis, Sénégal. (http://www.ceamitic.sn/)

References

[1] C. Diallo, M. Marot, and M. Becker, "Single-node cluster reduction in wsn and energy-efficiency during cluster formation," in Proc. of the 9th IFIP Annual Mediterranean Ad Hoc Networking Workshop, Med-Hoc-Net 2010, IEEE Communications Society, Juan-Les-Pins, France, June. 2010.

[2] A. D. de Clauzade de Mazieux, M. Marot, and M. Becker, "Correction, generalisation and validation of the "max-min d-cluster heuristic"," in Proc. of IFIP/TC6/LNCS NETWORKING, Atlanta, USA, May 2007.

[3] C. Diallo, M. Marot, and M. Becker, "Using lqi to improve clusterhead locations in dense zigbee based wireless sensor networks," in Proc. of the 6th IEEE International Conference on Wireless and Mobile Computing, Networking and Communications (WiMob 2010), Niagara Falls, Canada, October 2010.

[4] A. Amis, R. Prakash, T. Vuong, and D. Huynh, "Max-min d-cluster formation in wireless ad hoc networks," in 9th Annual Joint Conference of the IEEE Computer and Communications Societies, 2000.

[5] C. Diallo, M. Marot, and M. Becker, "A distributed link quality based d-clustering protocol for dense zigbee sensor networks," in Proc. of the third IFIP/IEEE Wireless Days International Conference, WD 2010, Venice, Italy, October 2010.

[6] D. Baker and A. Ephremides, "The architectural organization of a mobile radio network via a distributed algorithm," in IEEE Transactions on Communications, Vol. COM-29, No 11, pp. 1694-1701, Nov. 1981.

[7] A. Ephremides, J. Wieselthier, and D. Baker, "A design concept for reliable mobile radio networks with frequency hopping signaling," in Proceedings of IEEE, Vol. 75(1), pp. 56-73, 1987.

[8] J. Blumenthal, R. Grossmann, F. Golatowski, and D. Timmermann, "Weighted centroid localization in zigbee-based sensor networks," in IEEE International Symposium on Intelligent Signal Processing, WISP'07, 2007.

[9] M. Becker, A.-L. Beylot, R. Dhaou, A. Gupta, R. Kacimi, and M. Marot, "Experimental study: Link quality and deployment issues in wireless sensor networks," in Proc. NETWORKING'09, LNCS 5550, NETWORKING , Aachen, Germany, 2009, pp. 14–25.

[10] Tmote Sky datasheet., http://www.moteiv.com/products/docs/tmote-sky-datasheet.pdf.

[11] C. Radio, "http://www.chipcon.com," Last access, Mar. 2010.

[12] I. S. 802.15.4-2006, "Wireless medium access control (mac) and physical layer (phy) specifications for low-rate wireless personal area networks (wpans)," in IEEE Computer Society, 2006.

[13] Z. specification, "Zigbee specification v1," June 2005.

[14] S. S. World, "http://www.sunspotworld.com," Last access, Mar. 2010.

[15] E. W. S. Board, "http://www.easysen.com/wieye.htm," Last access, Mar. 2010.

Multi Objective Nodes placement Approach in WSN based on Nature Inspired Optimisation Algorithms

Faten Hajjej, Ridha Ejbali and Mourad Zaied
Research Laboratory in Intelligent Machines (REGIM-Lab)
Sfax, Tunisia
e-mail: {hajjej.faten.tn, ridha_ejbali, mourad.zaied }@ieee.org

Abstract—**The enormous demand of Wireless Sensor Networks (WSNs) in various applications has intensified the concern about sensor nodes placement. The choice of sensor deployment strategy is mentioned among the most critical issues for the designer of such networks. Some objective functions, such as coverage, energy consumption and network connectivity, are a key challenge that should be satisfied while achieving optimal placement topologies. In this work, deployment issue has been modeled as a constrained multi-objective optimization (MOO) problem. The aim of this work was to find the optimal sensor nodes positions in the area of interest in terms of coverage, energy consumption and network connectivity. A new multi-objective optimization approach based on Flower Pollination Algorithm (FPA) was introduced. The simulation results show that the proposed approach improve both coverage and energy consumption compared with other multi objective approaches.**

Keywords- **WSN;** ***Deployment Problem; Multi Objective Optimization; Energy Consumption; FPA.***

I. INTRODUCTION

Over the last few decades, fields of microelectronics, micromechanics and wireless communication technologies have made a noticeable progress that allows the production of cost-effective components of a few cubic millimeters in volume. Therefore, wireless sensor networks(WSNs) have arisen as a new area of research to provide more economical solutions , an easy to deploy remote monitoring and processing of data in complex environments, . WSNs consist of a large number of nodes deployed in a region of interest (RoI) to collect and transmit environmental data to one or more collection points autonomously. These networks are of interest especially for military applications, environmental applications, home automation, medical and many of the applications related to the surveillance of critical infrastructure. These applications often require a high level of security and characteristics sharing because of the lack of infrastructure, limited energy and dynamic topology. Sensor nodes have limited resources, namely the energy resources and the calculation capabilities as well as the storage capacity. Thus, most studies and researches on WSN have dealt with resources optimization problems in order to enhance the performances and meet the quality of service (QoS) requirements.

The deployment of a sensor in the RoI is a crucial issue for any WSN designers especially with the limitations of sensor nodes. In fact, WSN performances are greatly influenced by the placement strategies since they directly affect QoS metrics, such as energy consumption, sensor lifetime and sensing coverage equally [1]. Hence, a powerful sensor deployment strategy will obviously improve performance and resource management. The deployment strategies can be classified according to three criteria: the first is the placement methodology that can be either random placement or grid-based placement (deterministic placement).the second is the optimization of performance metrics such as connectivity, sensing coverage, energy consumption and lifetime. Finally, the roles the deployed node, which can be regular, relay, cluster-head, or base-station plays [2]. The placement techniques can be further categorized into static and dynamic according to whether the optimization is performed at the time of deployment or when the network is working, respectively. The choice of the deployment schema depends on many properties [2].

The coverage problem is one of the most basic issues in wireless sensor networks, it directly affects the capability and the performances of the sensor network [3]. The quality of coverage is immediately influenced by the choice of the deployment strategy. Most of the applications using WSN, especially those requiring permanent measurements collection, demand a low-energy consuming network. Also, for the sensors network itself, energy consumption is a critical issue since sensor nodes rely on limited power resources. As a result, an optimal deployment topology should achieve a trade-off between the coverage requirement and the energy constraint. In general, there exist conflicts between minimizing energy dissipation and maximizing coverage. To maximize the area of coverage, sensor nodes must be placed far away from the sink node (data collection point) which means that the sensor signals need higher power in order to reach farther distances. Multi-objective optimization approaches (MOOAs) are generally used to solve optimization problems with conflicting objectives. The multi-objective optimization (MOO) works on several objective function vectors simultaneously. Unlike, the single-objective optimization, the solution of MOO is a set of solutions, known as the set of pareto optimal solutions [4].

The connectivity metric in WSN is satisfied if, and only if, there exists at least one path between each pair of nodes. This requirement is at the same level of importance with the coverage requirement. Actually, these two metrics should be strongly related in order to ensure wider monitored area without connectivity holes.

Nature constantly inspires research in the field of optimization. While genetics, ants and particle swarm algorithms are famous examples, other nature inspired optimization algorithms emerge regularly. Flower Pollination Algorithm (FPA) is a novel global optimization algorithm inspired from pollination process of flowers. FPA is simple and very powerful; in fact, it can outperform both genetic algorithm (GA) and particle swarm optimization (PSO) according to [5].

In this work, we proposed a new deployment approach based on the multi objective version for FPA (MOFPA) [6] for WSN. Our approach aimed to find the optimal deployment topology taking into account the aforementioned objectives, i.e., minimizing energy consumption and maximizing total coverage while maintaining connectivity constraints.

The remainder of this paper is organized as follows. In Section 2, the related work is outlined. The problem formulation is presented in Section 3. Section 4 introduces the proposed approach. In Section 5, simulation results and discussion are given. Finally, Section 6 concludes the paper.

II. Related Work

Many literature surveys are available where optimization methods have been used to solve several nodes placement issues for WSNs. The authors in [7] proposed an improved version of Artificial Bee Colony algorithm to maximize the coverage rate in WSN. This algorithm modified the updating equation of onlooker bee and scout bee. In fact, some new parameters, such as forgetting, neighbor factor and probability of mutant were introduced to enhance coverage rate and accelerate the convergence speed. Sengupta et al. [8] achieved an optimal tradeoff between coverage, energy consumption and lifetime in WSN using the multi-objective evolutionary algorithm (MOEA). They developed an enhanced version of Multi-objective evolutionary algorithm based on differential evolution (MOEA/D-DE) known as MOEA/DFD, which includes the fuzzy dominance. The authors in [9] proposed three algorithms, specifically integer linear programming models, a local search algorithm and a genetic algorithm in order to solve the deployment problems of WSNs. Theirs approaches aimed at finding the optimal deployment in terms of area of coverage and number of wireless sensor nodes by taking into account the connectivity constraint. Likewise, they compared the three models with some regular sensor deployment patterns. The problem of the probability node deployment is less important than the distribution of the asymmetrical nodes. Zhang et al. [10] addressed the sensor nodes deployment issues for Directional Sensor Networks (DSNs). They proposed a novel placement approach based on PSO in order to enhance the coverage probability of the monitoring field. The probability coverage model was adapted as a sensing model.

III. Problem Formulation

Considering the severe resources constraints of sensor nodes and the levels of QoS required for the WSNs, an optimal placement process has to be considered. In this work, we aimed at finding the coordinates of the sensor nodes in a two-dimensional sensing area that insure the maximal coverage rate and minimal energy dissipation. The deployed sensors should be connected in an efficient way so that each deployed sensor can find a connection path to reach the sink node. Consequently, our deployment problem was modeled as a multi-objective optimization problem with two objective functions, namely total coverage ratio and energy consumption, and one problem constraint, namely the network connectivity.

A. Preliminary Definitions

Sensor nodes in WSN are characterized by their positions in the 2D plane (x, y), sensing radius R_s and communication radius R_c. Given a multi-hop WSN, where all nodes collaborate in order to ensure cooperative communication such network, can be defined as a linked graph, G = {V, E}, where V is the set of vertices representing sensors and E is the set of edges representing links between the sensors. Let u ϵ V and v ϵ V, (u, v) belongs to E if, and only if, u can directly send a message to v (we say that v is neighbor of u). We assume that R_c is identical for all nodes. Let d(u, v) be the distance between the nodes u and v, the set E can be defined as follows:

$$E = \left\{(u,v) \in V^2; \qquad d(u,v) \le R_c\right\}$$

The network coverage is defined by the sensing radius of the sensor node, whereas the network connectivity is specified by the communication radius of the nodes.

B. Multi objective optimization

Formulating an optimization problem as a multi objective problem is necessary in some cases, especially when the problem involves more than one objective functions and several constraints. The objective functions are typically conflicting; the task of MOOA is to find a tradeoff between the conflicted objectives. Unlike single-objective problem optimization, the results of MOOA are usually a set of solutions [4].

Definition 1. Multi-objective optimization problem

A multi-objective optimization problem is a problem of the following form:

$$\begin{cases} \text{Minimize/Maximize } f(x) = \left[f_1(x), f_2(x), \ldots f_n\right]^T \\ \text{Subject to } q_j(x) \ge 0, \qquad j=1, 2, \ldots, m, \\ h_d(x) = 0, \qquad d=1, 2, \ldots, l, \end{cases} \tag{1}$$

Where, xϵ E^n is the decision variables, n is the number of objective functions, l is the number of equality constraints and m is the number of inequality constraints [4].

Definition 2. *Pareto optimality*

MOO problem has actually many solutions in the feasible region that all fit a predetermined definition for an optimum solution. The predominant concept in defining an optimal

point is that of Pareto optimality. This is specified as follows:
A point, $y^* \epsilon Y$, is Pareto optimal if there is not another solution point $y \epsilon Y$, such that $f(y) \leq f(y^*)$ for at least one function [4].

Definition3. *Non-dominated solution*
A feasible solution is non-dominated if there is not another feasible solution better than the current one in some objective function.

C. *Energy Model*

The energy consumed by WSN is considered as the first objective function. Here, our purpose was to minimize the total energy consumed by the network. Supposing that E_0 is the initial energy capacity for each sensor and e_i is the energy consumed by each node i, e_i can be formulated as follows:

$$e_i = ME_i + TE_i \times P_{si} + RE_i \times \alpha_i \tag{2}$$

Where ME_i is the maintenance energy, TE_i is the transmission energy, Psi refers to the cost of minimum path from a sensor node i to the sink node, RE_i is the reception energy and α_i represents the number of sensors in which node i receives data and transfers it to the sink node in multi-hop communication.
The network total energy consumed is defined as the sum of the energy consumed by each node. So, our first objective function is given as follows:

$$f_1 = \text{Minimize}\left(\sum_{i=1}^{N_S} e_i \right) \tag{3}$$

With N the number of sensor nodes.

D. *Coverage Model*

Coverage in WSN can be defined as the total area covered by a collection of sensor nodes deployed in the region of interest (RoI). Coverage problems are commonly classified into two types: target coverage problem and area coverage problem. The former ensures the monitoring of only certain specific points which have fixed positions in the area of interest, while the latter is concerned with the supervision of the whole deployment area. In this paper, an area coverage problem was considered. The sensing area was considered as m × n grids, each grid point size was equal to 1 and denoted as G(x, y). The zone covered by a sensor node was a disk with a radius equal to the sensing radius of the sensor (R_s) (Figure 1). The binary sensing model was considered. For this model each grid point within the sensing radius of a node can be taken as covered with probability equal to "1" and point out of the sensing range was set as "0" since it cannot be covered.

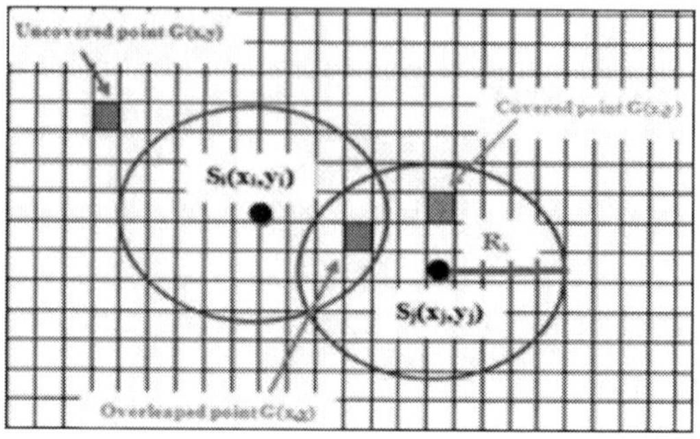

Figure 1. Sensor coverage in sensing field

Thus, the coverage of the whole area is proportional to the grid points that can be covered by at least one sensor $S_i(x_i, y_i)$ [17].

$$P(x, y, S_i) \begin{cases} 1, \text{ if } \sqrt{(x-x_i)^2 - (y-y_i)^2} \leq R_s \\ 0, \quad \text{otherwise} \end{cases} \tag{4}$$

Supposing that a WSN consists of N_S sensor nodes, the probability that a point G(x, y) is covered can be given by:

$$P(x,y,S) = 1 - \prod_{i=1}^{Ns} (1 - P(x,y,S_i)) \tag{5}$$

And the Coverage Ratio (R_{cov}) is given by:

$$R_{cov} = \frac{\sum_{x=1}^{m} \sum_{y=1}^{n} P(x,y,S)}{m * n} \tag{6}$$

The second objective function is to maximize the total coverage area. But, since energy consumption has to minimized, coverage metric should be modeled as a minimizing problem. So, our objective function has to be expressed as minimizing the non-coverage ratio which is equal to 0 in case of full coverage.

$$f_2 = \text{Minimize}(1 - R_{cov}) \tag{7}$$

E. *Connectivity Constraint*

The network connectivity is satisfied if there exists, at least, one path from the sensor node to the sink node. Here, connectivity is considered as a problem constraint.

Definition 1. *Node Degree*
Given an undirected graph G, the degree Deg (u) of a vertex $u \epsilon V$ is specified as the number of neighbors of u [11].

Definition 2. *k-Node Connectivity*
A graph is considered to be connected if for every pair of nodes, there exists a single hop or a multi-hop path connecting them otherwise the graph is called disconnected. A graph is considered to be Q-connected if for any pair of

nodes there are at least Q reciprocally separate paths connecting them [11].

IV. PROPOSED APPROACH

Our objective was to enhance the performances of WSN by optimizing both coverage [14] and energy consumption metrics without affecting the network connectivity. Here, we dealt with area coverage problem for a centralized random placement topology with a predefined number of sensors. The proposed approach is a multi objective approach based on FPA. This section presents the different rules and steps of the proposed approach.

A. Multi-Objective Flower Pollination Algorithm

Meta-heuristics algorithms are often inspired from nature and designed to solve challenging optimization problems. Here, we considered one of the most recent meta-heuristic algorithms named FPA, developed by Xin-She Yang in 2012 [5] for the global optimization problems. FPA inspired from the flower pollination process of flowering plants. In nature, flowers pollination process resulting from the transfer of pollen, typically, by pollinators such as insects, birds, bats and other animals. In this work, we presented a multi objective approach based on MOFPA [6] to solve deployment problems for WSN. FPA has the following four rules:

1. *Cross-pollination is a global pollination process with pollen carrying pollinators doing Lévy flights.*
2. *Self-pollination is considered as local pollination.*
3. *Flower constancy can be defined as the reproduction probability proportional to the similarity of the two flowers involved.*
4. *Global and local pollination is controlled by a switch probability $p \in [0, 1]$.*

The fitness function used for this work is given by the following equation:

$$f \quad \text{Minimize}(f_1, f_2) \qquad (8)$$

With f_1 and f_2 described above.

The pseudo code of the proposed approach is presented in Figure 2. Where N_f represents the number of flower, ε is the scaling factor, p is the switching probability, $\mathbf{F}^t_i$ is solution vector $\mathbf{F}_i$ at iteration t and g* is the current best solution found among all solutions at the current generation/iteration. Thus, to imitate the movement of the pollinator, FPA uses Lévy flight. Therefore, we draw $L > 0$ from a Lévy distribution:

$$L \sim \frac{\lambda \Gamma(\lambda) \sin(\frac{\pi \lambda}{2})}{\pi} \frac{1}{s^{1+\lambda}} \quad (s \square s_0 \square 0) \qquad (9)$$

```
Begin
Read N_s solution space, Max Iteration Max_T , ε, p, Iteration count
Tcount=0, and Flower count Fcount=0.

Step1: Create initial population of N_f Flowers F (Algorithm 2).
Step 2: Find fitness of each flower using f, then find the Global Flower g*
which have minimum fitness function value.
Step 3: For each flower except the g* generate a random number r.
  If (r<p) then
    Pollinate current flower with global flower g*:
    F_i^{t+1} ← F_i^t + L(g* + F_i^t)
  Else
    Pollinate current flower with any other flower in the population:
    F_i^{t+1} ← F_i^t + ε(F_k^t + F_j^t)
  End if
  F_count = F_count + 1
Step 4: if new solution F_i^{t+1} better than current solution then update them
in the population, if new solution F_i^{t+1} better than g* then update the
global solution.
Step5: if ( T_count < Max_T) then
T_count = T_count + 1
Else
Go to Step 3
End if
End
```

Figure 2. Pseudo-code of MOFPA

B. Initial population

To implement the proposed approach, we needed to create an initial population for FPA. In this work, we considered that each individual or flower represented the vector of all sensor nodes position (x, y) in RoI.

To create the initial population, we began by generating the position of the sink node at the centre of RoI for each flower. Then, we deployed the remaining sensors randomly after verifying the connectivity constraint. Actually, the network connectivity is assumed to be full if the distance between two sensors is less than the communication radius (Rc) of the sensor. Rc is set at $2R_S$ to guarantee the network connectivity [12]. The distance is defined as the Euclidean distance between two sensors. In addition, to ensure a sufficient distribution in RoI, we controlled the number of neighbors of each deployed node that should be less than a predefined number N_e. Here, N_e was set to 1. So, we dealt with 1-connected network.

The pseudo code of the initial population is presented in Figure 3. With S_i is the sensor node i, N_f is number of flowers, Rc is the node communication radius and N_e is the maximum number of neighbors.

```
Begin
Read Nf, Ns, Solution space , flower count Fcount=0, sensor count Scount=0,
Rc and neighbors Ne.

Step1: for each Flower F: Deploy (Sinki).
Step2: for each Flower F:
Scount=0
While ( Scount <=Ns )
Generate-Random-Position(Sk)
if ∃ Sj While Dkj < Rc then
  if Neighbors (Sk) ≤ Ne then
   Deploy(Sk)
   k←k+1
  End if
End if
End
```

Figure 3. Pseudo code of Initial Population Creation

V. SIMULATION AND RESULTS

To validate the performances of the proposed approach, some simulations were performed. Here, the binary sensing model was taken and sensor nodes of the initial population were randomly distributed.

TABLE I. DEFINITIONS AND VALUES OF SIMULATION PARAMETERS.

Parameter	Definition	Value
x_m	Maximum width of RoI	100m
y_m	Maximum length of RoI	100m
R_c	Communication radius	30 m
R_S	Sensing radius	15 m
N_S	Number of sensors	15
Ne	Maximum number of neighbours	1
IE	Initial energy for each sensor	1Ah
ME_i	Maintenance energy for node i	13 mA
TE_i	Transmission energy for node i	20 mA/m
RE_i	reception energy	2 mA
N_f	Number of flower	20
p	Switching probability	0.8
$NCov_{pop0}$	Non-coverage ratio of initial population	0.4777
E_{pop0}	Energy consumption of Initial population	8042 mA

The network is homogeneous, i.e., all sensors have the same deployment parameters such as the sensing and communication radius. Simulations were carried out using MATLAB R2016a. The algorithm was run a maximum number of iterations of 1500 for 5 runs.

Figure 4 presents all solutions (dominated and non-dominated) obtained over five runs of the proposed algorithms. The simulation shows that 90% of non-dominated solutions (see Figure 4) offered the following pairs of values: (217.09, 0.166) and (199.36, 0.168), for Energy Consumption and non-Coverage Ratio, respectively.

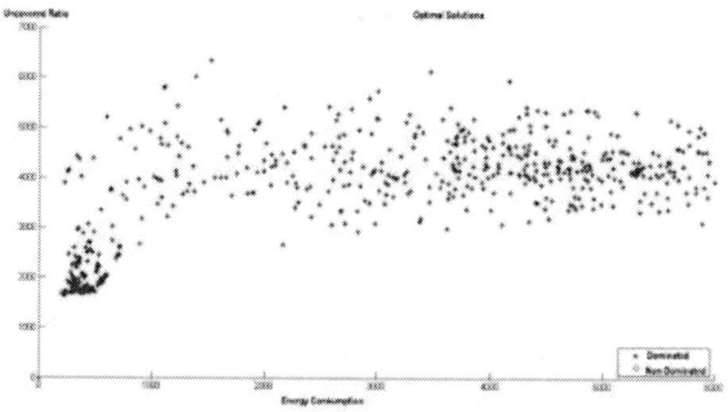

Figure 4. Non-Dominated Solutions of MOFPA

Tab I presents the definitions and the values of simulation parameters. The non-dominated solutions were close but not overlapping. Comparing the simulation results with the initial values, i.e. those of initial population, we can notice the amelioration offered by our approach in terms of the considered objective functions. Actually, the proposed approach was 38.62 and 2.86 times better in minimizing energy consumption and non-covered area, respectively.

In this work, the simulation results of MOFPA were compared with those of PSO algorithm [13] in different instances. PSO was tested by considering the same initial simulation parameters (See Tab I). Figure 5 and Figure 6 show the results of MOFPA compared with those of PSO algorithm.

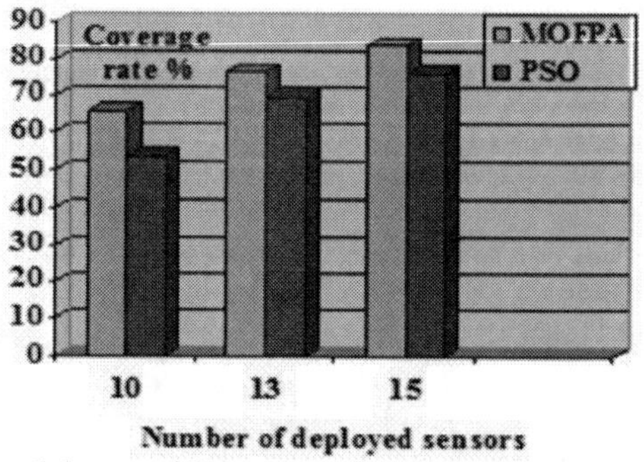

Figure 5. Average of Coverage rate of non-dominated solutions

Figure 5 presents the average of coverage rate of non-dominated solutions found after 1500 iterations of the two algorithms for different instances. We notice that the total coverage rate of RoI increases when the number of deployed nodes increases. The proposed approach outperforms the PSO in all instances and produces maximum coverage area.

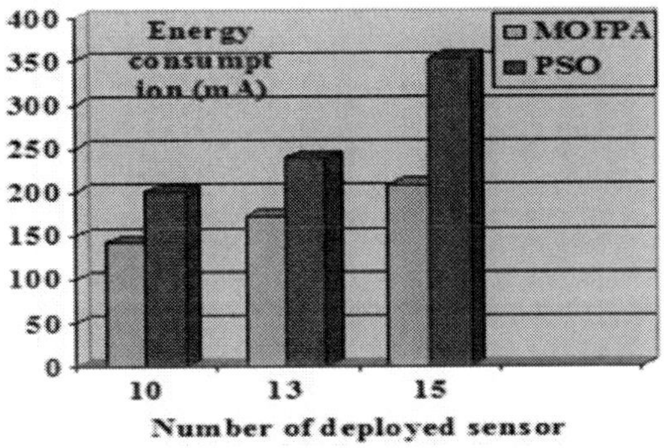

Figure 6. Average of energy measure of non-dominated solutions

Figure 6 presents the average of energy consumption of non-dominated solutions found after 1500 iterations of the two algorithms for different instances. We notice that the total energy consumption increases when the number of deployed nodes increases. The proposed approach outperforms the PSO in all instances and consumes minimum net energy.

VI. CONCLUSION

The multi-objective optimization algorithm aims to determine a set of optimal solutions which establish a trade-off between the different objective functions. This paper presented a new multi-objective approach for node deployment problem in WSN. The proposed approach tried to deploy sensor nodes in the RoI while maximizing coverage area, minimizing energy consumption and maintaining net connectivity. Simulation results prove that MOFPA out-performs PSO as it allows better network in terms of both coverage and energy consumption. In a future work, we will incorporate other QoS metrics like sensor lifetime.

REFERENCES

[1] F. Oldewurtel and P. Mhnen, "Analysis of enhanced deployment models for sensor networks," Vehicular Technology Conference (VTC 2010-Spring), May. 2010, pp. 1-5, doi: 10.1109/VETECS.2010.5494174.

[2] M. Younisa, and K. Akkayab, "Strategies and techniques for node placement in wireless sensor networks: A survey," Ad Hoc Networks. vol. 6, June. 2008, pp. 621-655, doi: 10.1016/j.adhoc.2007.05.003.

[3] S. Meguerdichian, F. Koushanfar, M. Potkonjak and M.B. Srivastava, "Coverage problems in wireless ad-hoc sensor networks," Twentieth Annual Joint Conference of the IEEE Computer and Communications Societies(INFOCOM 2001) , April. 2001, pp. 1380–1387, doi: 10.1109/INFCOM.2001.916633.

[4] R. T. Marler and J. S. Arora, "Survey of multi-objective optimization methods for engineering," Structural and Multidisciplinary Optimization, vol. 26, Mar. 2004, pp. 369–395, doi:10.1007/s00158-003-0368-6.

[5] X. S. Yang, "Flower pollination algorithm for global optimization," Unconventional Computation and Natural Computation, vol. 7445, Sep. 2012, pp.240-249, doi: 10.1007/978-3-642-32894-7_27.

[6] X. S. Yang, M. Karamanoglu and X. He, "Multi-objective flower algorithm for optimization," International Conference on Computational Science, 2013, pp. 861-868, doi: 10.1016/j.procs.2013.05.251.

[7] X. Yu, J. Zhang, J. Fan and T. Zhang, "A faster convergence artificial bee colony algorithm in sensor deployment for wireless sensor networks," International Journal of Distributed Sensor Networks, vol. 9, pp. 2-9, Oct. 2013, doi: 10.1155/2013/497264.

[8] S. Sengupta , S. Das, M. D. Nasir and B. K. Panigrahi, " Multi-objective node deployment in WSNs: In search of an optimal trade-off among coverage, lifetime, energy consumption, and connectivity", Engineering Applications of Artificial Intelligence, vol. 26, Jan. 2013, pp. 405-416, doi: 10.1016/j.engappai.2012.05.018.

[9] M. Rebai, M. L. berre, H. Snoussi, F. Hnaien and L. Khoukhi, "Sensor deployment optimization methods to achieve both coverage and connectivity in wireless sensor networks," Computers & Operations Research, vol. 59, Jul. 2015, pp. 11-21, doi: 10.1016/j.cor.2014.11.002.

[10] J. Zhang, Y. Lei, C. Chen and F. Lin, "Directional Probability Perceived Nodes Deployment Based on Particle Swarm Optimization," International Journal of Distributed Sensor Networks, vol. Apr. 2016, pp. 1-6, doi: 10.1155/2016/2046392.

[11] D. B. West, "Introduction to Graph Theory," 2nd ed., Prentice-Hall, Aug. 2003.

[12] A. Ghosh and S. K. Das, "Coverage and connectivity issues in wireless sensor networks: A survey", Pervasive and Mobile Computing," vol. 4, Jun. 2008, pp. 303–334, doi: 10.1016/j.pmcj.2008.02.001.

[13] R. Poli, J. Kennedy and T. Blackwell , "Particle swarm optimization," Swarm Intelligence, vol. 1, Jun. 2007, pp. 33-57, doi: 10.1007/s11721-007-0002-0.

[14] F. Hajjej, R. Ejbali and M. Zaied, " An efficient deployement approach for improved coverage in wireless sensor networks based on flower pollination algorithm," International Conference on Applications of Graph Theory in Wireless Ad hoc Networks and Sensor Networks (GRAPH-HOC), 2016, pp. 117– 129, doi: 10.5121/csit.2016.61511.

Hydrogen Peroxide Vapours Sensors Made From ZnO<La> and SnO_2<Co> Films

V. Aroutiounian, V. Arakelyan, M. Aleksanyan, A. Sayunts, G. Shahnazaryan
Department of Physics of Semiconductors and Microelectronics
Yerevan State University
Yerevan, Republic of Armenia
e-mail: kisahar@ysu.am

P. Kacer, P. Picha, J. A. Kovarik, J. Pekarek
Department of Organic Technology
University of Chemistry and Technology
Prague, Czech Republic
e-mail: Petr.Kacer@vscht.cz

B. Joost
Institute for Pharmaceutical Technology
Fachhochschule Nordwestschweiz,
Hochschule für Life Sciences
Muttenz, Switzerland
e-mail: berndt.joost@fhnw.ch

***Abstract*—Thin film hydrogen peroxide vapours sensors made from ZnO<La> and SnO_2<Co> were manufactured by the high-frequency magnetron sputtering method. Response of the prepared sensors was investigated at different concentrations of hydrogen peroxide vapours and temperatures of the sensor work body. It was found that the La-doped ZnO sensors exhibit a sufficient response at 10 ppm of hydrogen peroxide vapours at the operating temperature of 220 °C. Good response to 100 ppm of hydrogen peroxide vapours at the work body temperature of 150 °C was shown for Co-doped SnO_2 sensors.**

Keywords* - *sensor; hydrogen peroxide vapours; semiconductor; metal oxide; thin film.

I. Introduction

Hydrogen peroxide (H_2O_2) is used in such fields as medicine, pharmacology, food and textile industry due to a wide spectrum of its antibacterial properties, low toxicity, ecological purity (the residue of H_2O_2 decompose on neutral water and oxygen). However, insufficiently pure H_2O_2 in large concentrations under certain conditions (for example, in the presence of transition metals) can decompose fast and can be explosive. H_2O_2 is subsumed under the category of matters dangerous for man with certain maximum permissible concentration. Therefore, the correct selection of the H_2O_2 concentration during the sterilization of equipment technological surfaces and also control of the H_2O_2 content in the air after completion of disinfection cycle are very important. From this point of view, development and manufacturing of systems sensitive to H_2O_2, able to determine its concentration in the environment is a very actual problem and attracts interest of chemists, physicians, industrial engineers, etc.

Now the electrochemical sensors are wide used [1]-[3]. However, note that the process of chemical decontamination can be carried out in two different ways: the first is the wet approach using water or any other H_2O_2 solution and the second one is the dry method using H_2O_2 in vapour phase. Therefore, the development and manufacturing of stable and reproducible sensors sensitive to H_2O_2 vapours are required.

An H_2O_2 vapours phase checking is also crucially significant in connection with counterterrorism efforts. An amperometric sensor for detection of H_2O_2 vapours made of an agarose-coated Prussian-blue was investigated [4]. A single-wire optical sensor for H_2O_2 vapours was manufactured [5]. The chemiresistive films made of organic p-type semiconductors metalized phthalocyanines (MPcs, where M = p-, d-, and f-block elements) are also sensitive to H_2O_2 vapours [6].

The aim of the present paper is a development of the technology, manufacturing and investigation of solid-state H_2O_2 vapours sensors made from nanostructured semiconductor metal oxide films.

In Section I, the necessities in the development of the H_2O_2 sensors and, in particular, sensors sensitive to H_2O_2 vapours are briefly described. In Section II, the manufacture technology of sensors made from semiconductor doped with metal oxide ZnO<La> and SnO_2<Co> nanostructures is described. The results of investigations of its sensitivity to H_2O_2 vapours are presented. In Section III, the conclusions are made and the directions of the future work are described.

II. Experimental Results and Discussion

Ceramic targets made from ZnO doped with 1at.% La and SnO_2 doped with 2at.% Co were synthesized by the method of solid-phase reaction in air. The annealing was carried out at 1300 °C and 500 °C-1100 °C for the compacted samples of ZnO<La> and SnO_2<Co>, respectively.

Prepared semiconductor ZnO<La> and SnO_2<Co> targets with a diameter ~ 40 mm and thickness ~ 2 mm were used for deposition of nanosize films using the high-frequency magnetron sputtering method. Multi-Sensor-Platforms (purchased from TESLA BLATNÁ, Czech Republic) are used as substrates. The power of the magnetron generator unit was 60 W. Duration of the sputtering process was equal to 15 and 20 minutes for ZnO<La> and SnO_2<Co>, respectively. The sensing device was completed through the ion-beam sputtering deposition of palladium catalytic particles (the deposition time ~ 3 seconds). Further annealing of the manufactured structures in air was carried out at temperature 250 °C to obtain film homogeneity and eliminate mechanical stress.

The sensors manufactured by us are resistive, i.e., its operation is grounded on changes of resistance of gas sensitive semiconductor layer under the influence of H_2O_2 vapours caused by an exchange of charges between molecules of the semiconductor film and absorbed H_2O_2 vapours.

Response of prepared sensors made from doped metal oxide films under the influence of H_2O_2 vapours was measured using a home-made system [4]. Samples were placed in a hermetic chamber. A corresponding quantity of the H_2O_2 water solution with certain concentration was placed in the chamber to reach a required concentration of H_2O_2 vapours. Measurements of the manufactured sensors response were carried out at different concentrations of H_2O_2 vapours (from 10 ppm up to 4000 ppm). A platinum heater on a front side of the sensor ensures a necessary temperature of the work body. The sensor work body temperature was being varied from room temperature up to 350 °C.

The sensor resistance variance under the H_2O_2 vapours influence was measured using a special home-made computer program. A typical curve demonstrating changing of the sensor resistance under the influence of H_2O_2 vapours at invariable temperature of the work body is presented in Figure 1.

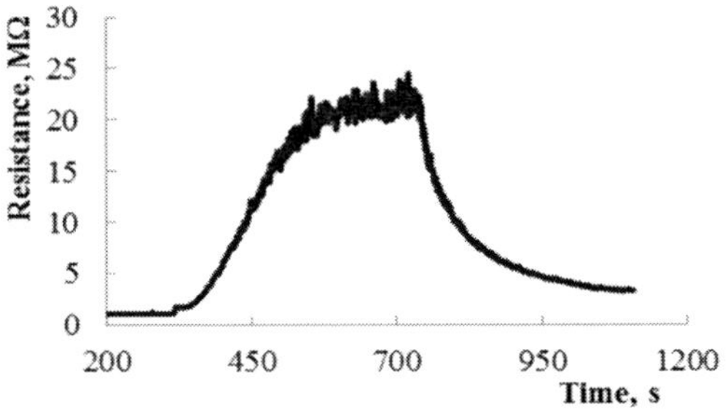

Figure 1. Resistance variation of the ZnO<La> sensor under the influence 1800 ppm of H_2O_2 vapours, work body temperature of 350 °C.

As a result of such measurements, the sensor response was determined as the ratio R_{vapors}/R_{air}, where R_{vapors} is the sensor resistance in the presence of H_2O_2 vapours in air and R_{air} is the sensor resistance in air without H_2O_2 vapours. The SnO_2<Co> sensor response to 100 ppm of H_2O_2 vapours at the work body temperature of 150 °C and 200 °C is presented in Figure 2. The temperature of the sensor work body remains constant during of the each measurement.

Investigations of the ZnO<La> sensors sensitivity to 10 ppm of H_2O_2 vapours were carried out at University of Chemistry and Technology (Prague). Firstly, an atmosphere containing 10 ppm of H_2O_2 vapours was prepared in a laboratory model of an isolator. This H_2O_2 vapours concentration decreased by spontaneous decomposition of H_2O_2. When a reference device (DrägerSensor® H_2O_2 HC) could not detect any H_2O_2 vapours, the sensor was inserted into the model isolator. Then, the sensor responded immediately. When the maximum response was reached, the sensor was taken out into an atmosphere without any traces of H_2O_2 vapours. This process was repeated three times. Results of these measurements are presented in Figure 3.

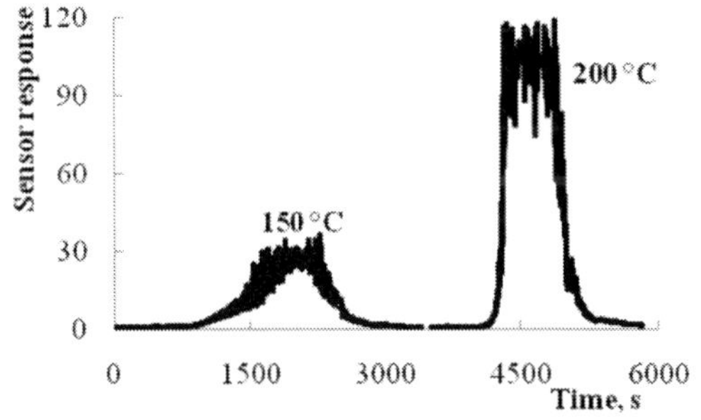

Figure 2. The SnO_2<Co> sensor response to 100 ppm of H_2O_2 vapours at different work body temperatures.

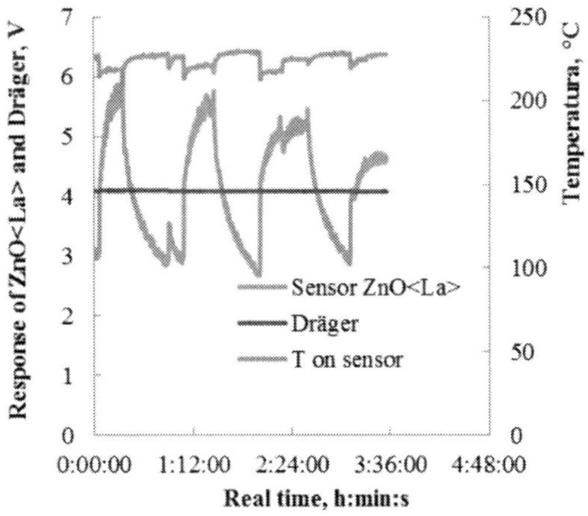

Figure 3. ZnO<La> sensors response to 10 ppm of H_2O_2 vapours.

Note that the DrägerSensor® H_2O_2 HC reference device is not sensitive to 10 ppm of H_2O_2 vapours. The ZnO<La> sensors were sufficiently sensitive to 10 ppm of H_2O_2 vapours at the work body temperature of 220°C, i.e. the sensors manufactured by us allow detection of H_2O_2 vapours concentrations which are not exceeding the maximum permissible value.

III. Conclusion and Future Work

The technology for semiconductor nanostructure sensors made from ZnO doped with 1at.% La and SnO_2 doped with 2at.% Co was developed. Specimen detecting H_2O_2 vapours were manufactured and investigated. Sensors made from ZnO<La> were sensitive to 10 ppm of H_2O_2 vapours. Sensors made from SnO_2<Co> exhibited good response to 100 ppm of H_2O_2 vapours at the operating temperature starting at 100°C. Our future work will be directed on the long-time stabilization of sensors parameters and the improvements of such characteristics as operation speed and recovery time.

ACKNOWLEDGMENT

This investigation was supported by the Swiss National Science Foundation FNSNF within the framework of the SCOPES DecoComp project.

REFERENCES

[1] W. Chen, S. Cai, Q.-Q. Ren, W. Wen, and Y.-D. Zhao, "Recent advances in electrochemical sensing for hydrogen peroxide: a review", Analyst, vol. 137, pp. 49-58, January 2012, doi:10.1039/c1an15738h.

[2] X. Yang et. al., "Size controllable preparation of gold nanoparticles loading ongraphene sheets@cerium oxide nanocomposites modified goldelectrode for nonenzymatic hydrogen peroxide detection", Sensors and Actuators B, vol. 238, pp. 40-47, January 2017, doi:10.1016/j.snb.2016.07.016.

[3] Z.-L. Wu, C.-K. Li, J.-G. Yu, and X.-Q. Chen, "MnO_2/reduced graphene oxide nanoribbons: Facile hydrothermal preparation and their application in amperometric detection of hydrogen peroxide", Sensors and Actuators B, vol. 239, pp. 544-552, February 2017, doi:10.1016/j.snb.2016.08.062.

[4] J. Benedet, D. Lu, K. Cizek, J. La Belle, and J. Wang, "Amperometric sensing of hydrogen peroxide vapor for security screening", Anal. Bioanal. Chem., vol. 395, pp. 371–376, April 2009, doi:10.1007/s00216-009-2788-7.

[5] J. Y. Zheng et al., "Hydrogen peroxide vapor sensing with organic core/sheath nanowire optical waveguides", Adv. Mater., vol. 24, pp. OP194–OP199, July 2012, doi:10.1002/ adma.201200867.

[6] F. I. Bohrer et al., "Selective detection of vapor phase hydrogen peroxide with phthalocyanine chemiresistors", J. Am. Chem. Soc., vol. 130, pp. 3712-3713, December 2008, doi:10.1021/ja710324f

[7] V. M. Aroutiounian et al., "Study of the surface-ruthenated SnO_2/MWCNT nanocomposite thick- film gas sensors", Sensors and Actuators B, vol. 177, pp. 308-315, February 2013, doi:10.1016/j.snb.2012.10.10.

Comparison between MOX sensors for low VOCs concentrations with interfering gases

Frank James, Tomas Fiorido, Marc Bendahan, Khalifa Aguir
Aix Marseille Université, CNRS, Université de Toulon, IM2NP- UMR 7334, Marseille, France

email : frank.james@im2np.fr
email : tomas.fiorido@im2np.fr
email : marc.bendahan@im2np.fr
Corresponding author, email: khalifa.aguir@im2np.fr

***Abstract*—N-type Metal Oxide (MOX) sensors was developed to detect Volatile Organic Compounds (VOCs) at low concentration level. Sensitive layer like SnO_2, ZnO and WO_3 was deposited by reactive RF sputtering method. The sensors is based on a micro heater and a MOX sensitive layer on a silicon substrate. Gas sensing properties have been investigated toward isobutylene, as a typical VOC. The optimum working temperature was experimentally determined at 285°C for isobutylene. This work highlights the detection of VOC with interfering gas by MOX sensor at low level. This sensor will be used for a real time indoor air monitoring.**

Keywords: gas sensor, MOX sensor, isobutylene, carbon dioxyde, carbone monoxyde.

I. INTRODUCTION

Some MOX sensors are investigated in order to detect VOCs thanks to their miniaturization and real-time monitoring capabilities. In this work, we have chosen three main n-type metal oxide used in this field: SnO_2 [1], WO_3 [2], and ZnO [3]. The aim of the comparison between the performances of these sensitive materials is to find the best sensitive layer for our low VOCs concentrations sensors and to evaluate the effect of interfering gases like CO and CO_2. In the Section 2, we will describe the sensitive layers and the sensor and in the Section 3 we will highlight the main results of this work.

II. MATERIAL AND METHODS

A. *Sensitive layer*

The three sensitive thin layers (~50nm) under study are deposited by reactive magnetron RF sputtering and annealed at 450°C during 1h30 to improve their Nano-crystallization and the stability of the sensors response. Fig.1 shows the XRD patterns of the three thin film. All the diffraction peaks show tetragonal rutile structure for SnO_2, monoclinic structure for WO_3 and hexagonal structure for ZnO (JCPDS cards No 72-1147, 41-1445, 36-1451 respectively).

Under isobutylene, the reducing molecules will react with the adsorbed oxygen ions and release the trapped electrons back to the metal oxide conduction band. This reaction leads to the decrease of electron depletion barrier and to increase the electrical conduction of the metal oxide.

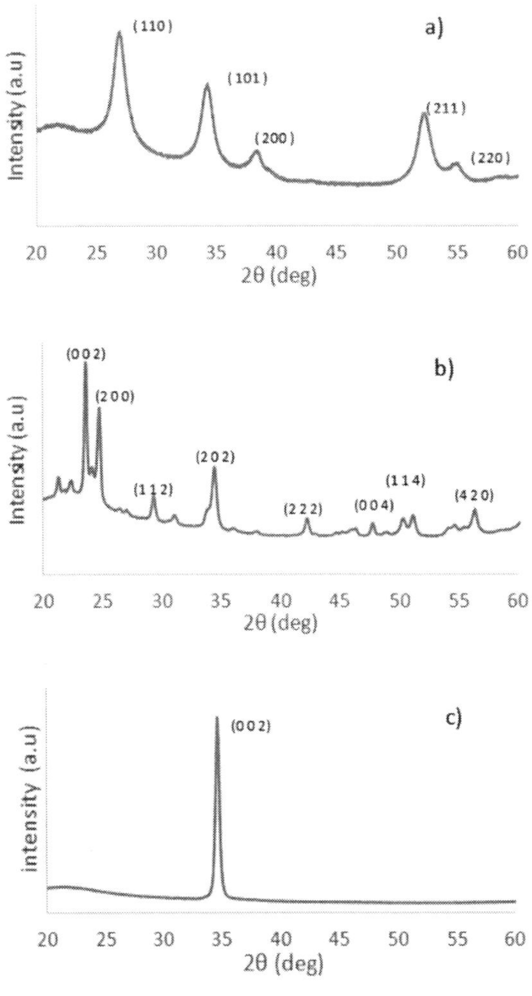

Figure 1. XRD patterns of a) SnO_2, b)WO_3 and c) ZnO made by reactive RF sputtering

B. *Chip gas sensor*

The gas sensors fabricated with SnO_2, WO_3 and ZnO layers as sensitive material is presented in Fig.2.

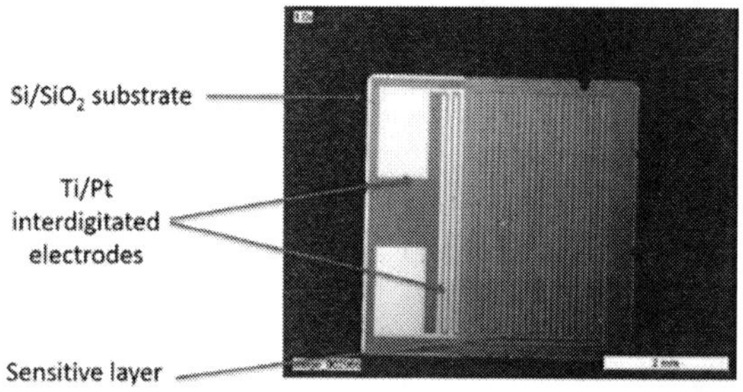

Figure 2. MOX Sensor with Si/SiO_2 substrate

This device has been tested with an automated gas bench with isobutylene. We used a power supply to control the operating temperature and a source meter for the data acquisition. This target gas was injected into a dilution system with or without interfering compounds. The outline was connected to a thermo-regulated test chamber. For each concentration, the sensor was exposed to isobutylene for 1 min then to dry air during 10 min. The sensors were maintained at the nominal heating voltage in dry air until the baseline was obtained to reach the response [4] under a flow rate of 500 sccm.

III. RESULTS AND DISCUSIION

A. *Response to isobutylene*

Fig.3 shows a typical responses with a wide range of detection from 50 ppb to 500 ppb of isobutylene. The best working temperature has been determined at 285°C.

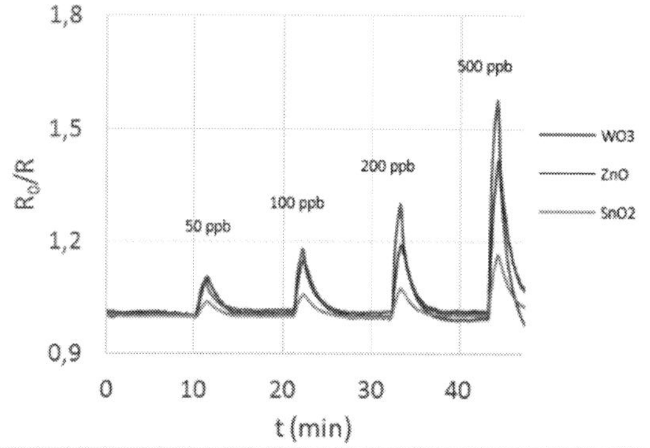

Figure 3. Sensors response for isobutylène concentrations, from 50 ppb to 500 ppb.

WO_3 and ZnO sensors seem to be the best devices for isobutylene. We have reached the highest responses from the three sensitive layer with low concentrations.

B. *Influence of interfering gases*

We have chosen 10 ppm of CO and 1% CO_2 as interfering gases concentrations. The Fig.4 shows the comparison of the responses of the three materials and for the two gases.

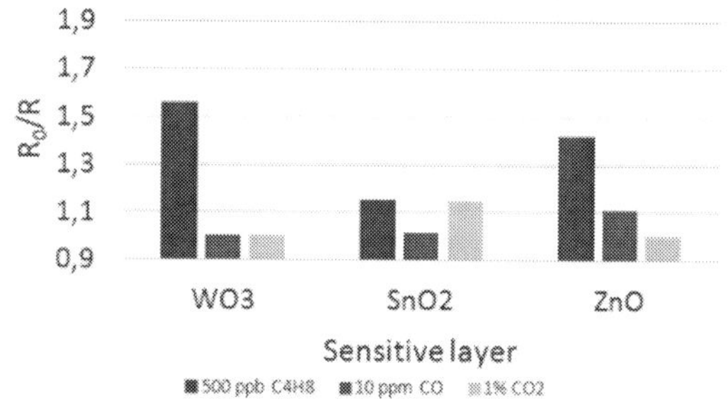

Figure 4. Sensor response under isobutylene and interferring gases

WO_3 and SnO_2 show low responses towards CO and CO_2 despite the better response for the target gas.

With tests under the same experimental conditions we can classify the right metal oxide for a target gas like isobutylene in presence of interferring gases.

IV. CONCLUSION

The gas measurement showed fast response / recovery times towards isobutylene. The best sensitive layers are WO_3 and ZnO because we have the highest responses for isobutylene and the weakest influence towards gases like CO and CO_2. This is the first step for air gas monitoring. We want to improve the selectivity towards others VOCs like benzene and toluene. On the other hand and after identifying the appropriate sensitive materials, we plan to study the improvement of the selectivity of these sensors.

ACKNOWLEDGMENTS

The authors would like to thank Antoine Dumas from EcologicSense Rousset – France, a company specialized in Diagnostics & Monitoring environments, SATT Sud Est a technology transfer accelerator company and Mr. A. Combes for his technical support in this work.

REFERENCES

[1] Z. Tang , G. Jiang, P. C. H. Chan, J. K. O. Sin, S. S. Lau , Theory and experiments on r.f. sputtered tin oxide thin-films for gas sensing applications, Sensors and Actuators B vol. 43, pp. 161-164, 1997.

[2] M. Bendahan, R. Boulmani, J.L. Seguin, K. Aguir , Characterization of ozone sensors based on WO_3 reactively sputtered films: influence of O_2 concentration in the sputtering gas and working temperature, Sensors and Actuators B, Chemical vol. 100, pp. 320-324, 2004.

[3] V. Senay et al., ZnO thin film synthesis by reactive radio frequency magnetron sputtering, Applied Surface Science vol. 318, pp. 2-5, 2014.

[4] C. Wang, L. Yin, L. Zang, D. Xiang, and R. Gao, Metal oxide gas sensors: Sensitivity and influencing factors, Sensors, vol. 10, pp. 2088-2106, 2010

Studies of Resistive-type Hydrogen-Sensitive Sensors Using Pd-Based Thin Films

Hao Lo, Chieh Lo
Graduate Institute of Electronics Engineering
National Taiwan University
Taipei, Taiwan
e-mail: hao291475@gmail.com
e-mail: a0937869023@gmail.com

Jian-Hong Wu, Wen-Shiung Lour
Department of Electrical Engineering
National Taiwan Ocean University
Keelung, Taiwan
e-mail: jhwu@gmail.com
e-mail: wslo@mail.ntou.edu.tw

***Abstract*—Zigzag-shaped Pd-based thin films (pure Pd and Pd-SiO_2 mixture with thickness ranged from 10 nm to 100 nm deposited on cover-glass substrates were used to fabricate resistive-type hydrogen sensors. It is found that relative sensitivities are independent of the thin-film thickness and are 10%, 7.4%, 6.1%, and 5% for the pure-Pd sensor in 2%, 1.5%, 1%, and 0.5% H_2/N_2, respectively. However, its response time (t_a) is substantially influenced by the thin-film thickness for pure-Pd resistive-type sensor. t_a is measured with a thickness coefficient of 0.14 s/nm in 2% H_2/N_2 while it is 0.5 s/nm in 1% H_2/N_2. Compared to the pure-Pd sensor, the Pd-SiO_2 sensor has a shorter response time (20 s to 33 s) and a higher relative sensitivity (8.7% to 6.1%) in 1% H_2/N_2. In 3% H_2/N_2, relative sensitivity is even as high as 15.2% with a response time of 10 s.**

Keywords-hydrogen; resistive-type; sensitivity; sensorr

I. Introduction

Hydrogen has attracted attention as a clean energy carrier. However, it is volatile and explosive. Thus, a lot of efforts have been made to search for high performance hydrogen sensors to monitor hydrogen leak. This is required not only for better control of hydrogen-involved processes but also for health and safety. Various types of semiconductor hydrogen sensors have been reported [1]-[6]. Among them, resistive-type sensors with Pd thin film have been reported to give good H_2 sensitivity. Previous studies reveal that the sensing behavior is of two types, depending on whether the electric resistance is increased or decreased upon exposure to H_2. Our previous work [6] also concluded that the resistive-type sensor with the Pd-SiO_2 thin-film mixture exhibits much better sensing performance than that with the pure-Pd thin film did. However, the sensor reversibility was evaluated using testing gases with hydrogen concentration below 1% in N_2. In addition, a fixed 30 nm Pd-SiO_2 thin-film mixture or pure-Pd thin film was employed. No further effect of thin-film thickness on sensitivity and response time was investigated. In this work, the Pd-SiO_2 thin-film mixture was again successfully deposited upon a robust and low-cost cover-glass substrate. Various hydrogen-containing gases with concentration up to 3% in N_2 were used to study its sensing properties that will be compared to those of the pure-Pd thin-film. Besides, thin films with thickness ranged from 10 nm to 100 nm were also employed in the fabrication of resistive-type sensors. Effects of thin-film thickness on sensitivity and response time were then investigated. It is found from experimental results that the Pd-SiO_2 thin-film mixture really exhibits better sensing performance than that of the pure-Pd thin film. Experiments and measurements about the proposed resistive-type hydrogen sensor are described in following section. In Section III, experimental results including key merits, such as sensitivity and response time, are addressed. Finally, conclusions are drawn in Section IV.

II. Experiments

Thin films of a pure Pd and a Pd-SiO_2 mixture were deposited on 18 mm × 18 mm × 0.17 mm cover-glass substrates by a thermal evaporator equipped with multiple tungsten boats. The background pressure of the thermal evaporator for deposition was 2×10^{-7} torr. The pure-Pd thin film was deposited at the rate of 72 nm /min. The Pd-SiO_2 mixture was deposited by co-evaporating Pd and SiO_2 at the rate of 80 nm /min. The thickness of the deposited thin film was monitored by a quartz crystal head real time. Fig. 1 shows geometric dimension of the resistive-type sensor fabricated in a zigzag-shaped microstructure with a total length of 53 mm. The cross-sectional area which the current flows through is 50 μm × t nm where t is the thickness of the deposited thin film. The sensing area of the resistive-type sensor is 53 mm × 50 μm. Since no other metals are required, our Pd-SiO_2 resistive-type sensor could be fabricated in a simple manner and at low cost. Besides, we found that surface morphologies between the pure-Pd and the Pd-SiO_2 thin films are quite different. That is, the Pd-SiO_2 thin film is indicative of porous-like morphology [7]-[8]. Hydrogen

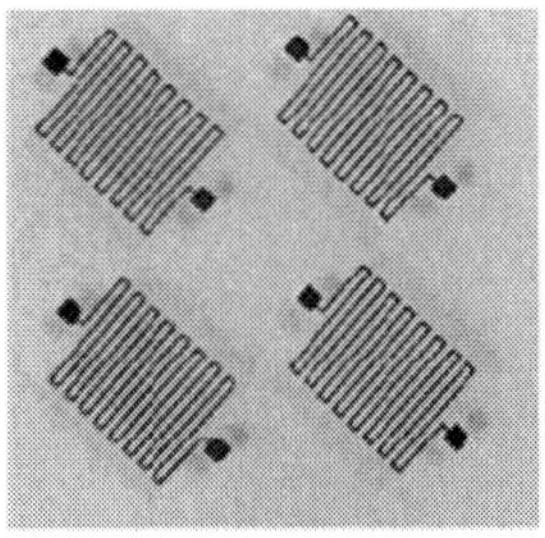

Figure 1. Schematic image of the Pd-based thin film used as a resistive-type hydrogen sensor with a sensing area of 53 mm × 50 μm.

detection was carried out using a custom-made flow-through test chamber made from stainless steel. A 500 ml/min constant flow N_2 was used as the carrier gas to achieve a baseline. It allows controlling the gas flow from N_2 to gas mixtures with various concentrations of 100 ppm to 3% H_2/N_2. The use of H_2 in N_2 is to realize the role of oxygen species on absorbing H atoms. Current-transient responses were measured by mounting the resistive-type sensors on a test fixture and using a semiconductor parameter analyzer. Then the dynamic current at a constant voltage and hence the electric resistance change recorded every 5 s were obtained as sensing signals.

III. RESULTS AND DISCUSSION

Fig. 2 shows the transient current response of the pure-Pd sensor to the introduction and removal of various hydrogen-containing gases biased at 2 V. In a N_2 ambience, a resistivity of 1.66×10^{-5} Ω·cm was measured according to a thin-film thickness of 16 nm together with the zigzag-shaped dimension. When the pure-Pd thin film is exposed to a hydrogen-containing gas, hydrogen molecules are dissociated into hydrogen atoms, which are absorbed in the interstitial sites of the Pd lattice. The electric-resistance increment and hence the increase in resistivity can be attributed to carrier scattering due to the incorporated hydrogen atoms. On the contrary, by replacing the hydrogen-containing gas with N_2, desorption of hydrogen atoms gives rise to the reduction of the resistivity of the pure-Pd thin film. Then, the relative sensitivity (S_H) is obtained according to experimental results shown in Fig. 2. It is found that S_H are

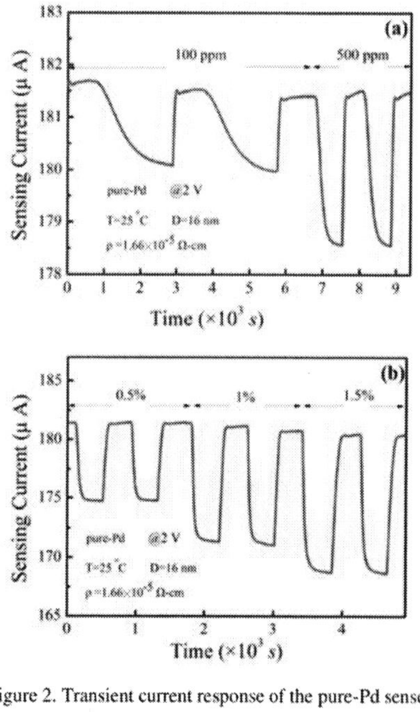

Figure 2. Transient current response of the pure-Pd sensor.

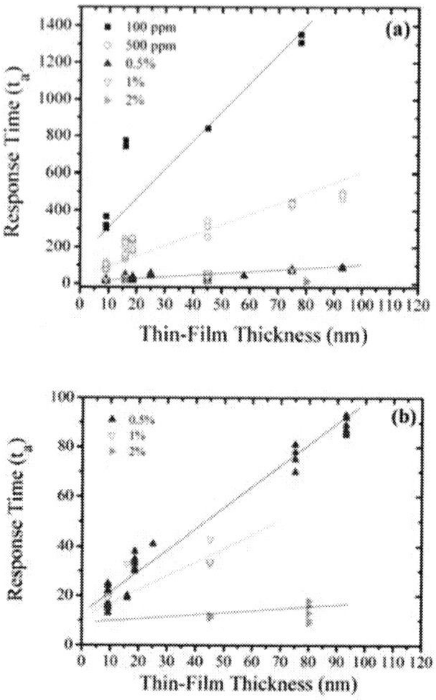

Figure 3. Reponse time versus thin-film thickness for a pure-Pd sensor.

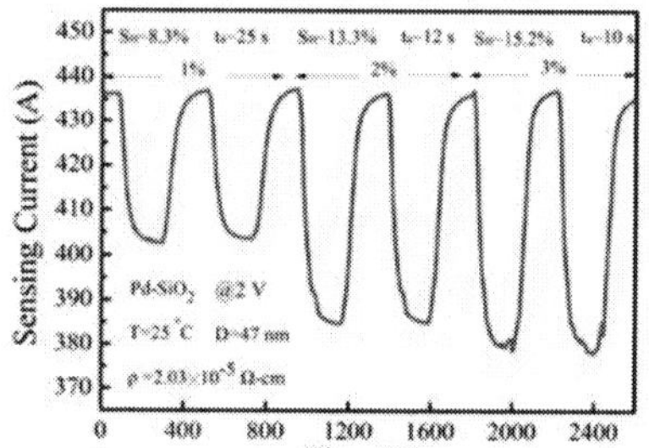

Figure 4. Transient current response of the $Pd\text{-}SiO_2$ sensor.

7.4% and 6.1% for the pure-Pd sensor in 1.5% and 1% H_2/N_2, respectively. No clear correlation was found between the relative sensitivity and the thin-film thickness. However, as shown in Fig. 3, the response time (t_a) as a function of thin-film thickness for a pure-Pd sensor subjected to 100 ppm to 2% H_2/N_2, we find it is substantially dependent on the thin-film thickness. For example, t_a with a thickness coefficient of 0.14 s/nm in 2% H_2/N_2 was obtained while it is 0.5 s/nm in 1% H_2/N_2. Fig. 4 shows sensing characteristics of the $Pd\text{-}SiO_2$ sensor. The baseline current in N_2 is 436.2 μA responding to a resistivity of 2.03×10^{-5} Ω·cm. The high resistivity is due to incorporation of insulating SiO_2. The current variation is more substantial when the gas with a higher hydrogen concentration is introduced to the $Pd\text{-}SiO_2$ sensor. This is because that the resistivity increased in the sensing film is proportional to the H_2 concentration in the sensing film. Since more hydrogen molecules coming to the sensing film can be dissociated into hydrogen atoms, more hydrogen atoms can diffuse into and locate inside the sensing film. It is thus easily demonstrated that the hydrogen concentration in the sensing film is enhanced by introducing hydrogen-containing gas with a high concentration. A typical response time of 12 s and $S_H \approx 13.3\%$ is obtained for the Pd-SiO_2 resistive-type hydrogen sensor in 2% H_2/N_2. We measured the high hydrogen concentrations 3% H_2/N_2. There is a better performance of $S_H \approx 15.2\%$ and $t_a \approx 10$ s.

IV. Conclusions

Pd-based resistive-type hydrogen sensors were reported with new findings include at least that (i) response time is substantially dependent on the thin-film thickness and (ii) SiO_2 incorporated into Pd thin film is useful for increasing sensitivity and shortening response time. However, studies of effects of the mole fraction of SiO_2 incorporated into the Pd film on the sensor's sensitivity and response time are undergoing to obtain low-cost and high-performance hydrogen sensors.

Acknowledgment

This work was financially supported by the Ministry of Science and Technology under contract no. MOST 104-2221-E-019-021-MY2.

References

[1] W. C. Liu et al., "Hydrogen Sensitive Characteristics of a Novel Pd/InP MOS Schottky Diode Hydrgeon Sensor," IEEE Trans. Electron Devices, vol. 48, pp. 1938-1944, 2001.

[2] A. Salchi, A. Nikfarjam, and D. J. Kalantari, "Pd/porous-GaAs Schottky Contact for Hydrogen Sensing Application," Sens. Actuators B, vol. 113, pp. 419-427, 2006.

[3] J. Schalwig et al., "Hydrogen Response Mechanism of Pt-GaN Schottky Diodes," Appl. Phys. Lett., vol. 80, pp. 1222-1224, 2002.

[4] S. Y. Chiu et al., "High-Sensitivity Metal-Semiconductor-Metal Hydrogen Sensors with a Mixture of Pd and SiO_2 Forming Three-Dimensional Dipoles," IEEE Electron Device Lett., vol. 29, pp. 1328-1331, 2008.

[5] C. Lo et al., "Unidirectional Sensing Characteristics of Structured Au-GaN-Pt Diodes for Differential-Pair Hydrogen Sensors," Int. J. Hydrogen Energy, vol. 37, pp. 18579-18587, 2012.

[6] C. Lo, S. W. Tan, C. Y. Wei, J. H. Tsai, and W. S. Lour, "Sensing Properties of Resistive-Type Hydrogen Sensors with a Pd-SiO_2 Thin-Film Mixture," Int. J. Hydrogen Energy, vol. 38, pp. 313-318, 2013.

[7] C. H. Huang et al., "Hydrogen Sensors with Pd Nanoparticles up an Interfacial Layer with Oxygen," Appl. Phys. Exp., vol. 3, pp. 075001-1-075001-3, 2010.

[8] S. W. Tan, J. H. Tsai, S. W. Lai, C. Lo, and W. S. Lour, "Hydrogen-Sensitive Sensor with Stabilized Pd-Mixture Forming Sensing Nanoparticles on an Interlayer," Int. J. Hydrogen Energy, vol. 36, pp. 15446-15454, 2011.

Study of Propylene Glycol and Dimethylformamide Vapors Sensors Based on MWCNTs/SnO_2 Nanocomposites

Zaven Adamyan, Artak Sayunts, Vladimir Aroutiounian, Emma Khachaturyan, Arsen Adamyan
Yerevan State University, Department of Physics of Semiconductors and Microelectronics
YSU
Yerevan, Armenia
e-mail: kisahar@ysu.am

Martin Vrnata, Přemysl Fitl, Jan Vlček
University of Chemistry and Technology, Department of Physics and Measurement Technology
UCT
Prague, Czech Republic
e-mail: martin.vrnata@vscht.cz

***Abstract*—We present results of our research works related to the study of thick-film multiwall carbon nanotube/tin oxide nanocomposite sensors of propylene glycol (PG) and dimethylformamide (DMF) vapors derived using hydrothermal synthesis and sol-gel methods. Investigations of response/recovery characteristics in the 50-300°C operating temperature range reveal that the optimal operating temperature for PG and DMF vapor sensors, taking into account both high response and acceptable response and recovery times, are about 200 and 220°C, respectively. A sensor response dependence on gas concentration in both cases is linear. The minimal propylene glycol and dimethylformamide gas concentrations at which the perceptible signal was registered by us were 13 ppm and 5 ppm, respectively.**

Keywords-MWCNTs/SnO₂; gas; vapor; sensor; dimethylformamide; propylene glycol.

I. Introduction

There are various harmful and hazardous matter vapors, which have a major role in diverse spheres such as environmental protection, industrial manufacture, medicine, as well as national defense. As an illustration, propylene glycol (PG) is an excellent solvent for many organic compounds and is used as an active ingredient in engine coolants and antifreeze, brakes, paints, enamels and varnishes, and in many products as a solvent or surfactant. It can also be found in cosmetics, perfumes, as well as in pharmaceuticals.

Another example is the dimethylformamide (DMF) which is used as a solvent in vinyl resins, adhesives, pesticide and epoxy formulations; which purifies and separates of acetylene, 1,3-butadiene, acid gases and aliphatic hydrocarbons, also in the production of polyacrylic or cellulose triacetate fibres and pharmaceuticals or in the production of polyurethane resin for synthetic leather [3].

DMF and PG have a huge impact on human organs (e.g. liver, skin, eyes and kidneys [1]-[3]). PG can cause nausea and vomiting, headache, dizziness and fainting. Moreover, it is known as a combustible liquid, which can explode in fire.

Due to the information noted above, PG and DMF gas sensors have a huge application for detecting and continuous monitoring of these gases, in the spheres where they are used. As a result of our carefully conducted analysis of the literature data, we did not find any works related to research and development of resistive sensors of PG and DMF gases. There are only sensors working in other principle (for example sensors working on modification of color of the substance), which is incompatible for contemporary technic, while, resistive gas sensors made from metal oxides have advantages such as electric signal, measurement of concentration, small sizes, low power consumption, high sensitivity, and long reliability [4]-[6].

Nanomaterials, as carbon nanotubes (CNTs), metal-oxide nanoparticles, nanotubes, nanowires and other various nanopatterns formation [7]-[12] are widely used in gas sensings for their excellent responsive characteristics, mature preparation technology, and low cost of mass production. Due to the covering of CNTs walls with metal-oxide nanoparticles, specific surface area of such gas-sensitive nanocomposites increases more. Moreover, nanochannels in the form of hollows of CNTs promote penetration of gas molecules deeper down in the nanocomposite sensitive layer [13]. Hence, it can be expected that application in gas sensors technology of nanocomposite structures composed of metal oxide functionalized with CNTs should enhance the gas sensor parameters, such as gas response, response, recovery times, and operating temperatures.

Our recent works related to the study of gas sensors based on multiwall carbon nanotubes/tin oxide (MWCNTs/SnO_2) nanostructures are also argued in [10] [14] [15]. The choice of tin oxide as a component of SnO_2/MWCNTs nanocomposite structure is conditioned by the fact that SnO_2 is well known and studied basic material for metal-oxide gas sensors (see, for example [4] [9] [16] [17]). We expected that coating of functionalized MWCNTs with SnO_2 nanoparticles with admissible, (close to double Debay length) sizes [16]-[20] should provide the improved performance of the gas sensor and lowered temperature of its operating

Here, we present the characteristics of the PG and DMF vapor sensors based on ruthenated thick-films MWCNT/SnO_2 nanocomposite structures. The choice of corresponding processing technique, treating conditions and regimes for CNTs functionalization, as well as modification of thick films surface with Ru catalyst, are described below in the second section. Results of the measurements of PG and DMF vapor sensors and their discussions are given in the third section.

II. EXPERIMENTAL DEVELOPMENT

MWCNTs/SnO_2 nanocomposite material processing and thick-film sensor manufacturing technology on the base of this nanocomposite are presented in this section. It is shortly described both the MWCNTs preparation and its covering with SnO_2 nanoparticles obtained by using the hydrothermal method. Ruthenium catalyst deposition technology is also shown here.

A. Material preparation

Firstly, MWCNTs were prepared by the decomposition of acetylene (CVD method) using Fe, Co/$CaCO_3$ catalyst [21] [22]. Such growth procedure using $CaCO_3$ catalyst enables a highly efficient selective formation of clean MWCNTs, suitable for effective bonding between CNT and metal-oxide, particularly, for SnO_2 precursors.

The preparation of nanocomposite materials with a hydrothermal method was carried out in two steps. Firstly, purified MWCNTs were dispersed in water via sonication. Then, a calculated amount of precursor of the $SnCl_2{\bullet}2H_2$ was dissolved in another beaker in water, whereupon 3 cm^3 HCl was added to the solution. In the next step, the MWCNT's suspension and the solution of the precursor were mixed and sonicated for 30 min. For preparing the nanocomposites, we poured the above-mentioned solutions into autoclaves, where hydrothermal synthesis was carried out at 150°C for 1 day. At the end of this procedure, all obtained nanocomposite powders were filtered and dried at 90°C for 5h. The final mass ratios of the nanocomposite MWCNT/SnO_2 obtained with the hydrothermal method in this study were 1:200, respectively. The hydrothermal synthesis process is presented in details in [10] [23].

B. Samples

The paste for the thick film deposition made by mixing powders with α-terpineol ("Sigma Aldrich") and methanol was printed on the chemically treated surface of the alumina substrate over the ready-made Pt interdigitated electrodes. The thin-film Pt heater was formed on the back side of the substrate. Then, the obtained composite structures were cut into 3×3 mm pieces. After that, the drying and annealing processes of the resulting thick films were carried out in two stages: The first step is the heating of thick films up to 220°C with $2^oC{\times}min^{-1}$ rate of temperature rise and holding for 3h and then increasing in temperature until 400°C with $1^oC{\times}min^{-1}$ rate and holding for 3h. In the second step, the thick-film specimens were cooled down in common with the oven.

After annealing and cooling processes, the surface of MWCNTs/SnO_2 thick films was ruthenated by dipping samples into the 0.01M $RuOHCl_3$ aqueous solution for 20min whereupon drying at 80°C for 30 min. Then, the annealing treatment was carried out again by the same method noticed above. The choice of the ruthenium as a catalyst was determined by its some advantages [10] [15] [23]. At the final stage, ruthenated MWCNT/SnO_2 chips were arranged in TO-5 packages and the gas sensors would be ready to measurements after bonding of leads.

III. RESULTS AND DISCUSSIONS

Some results of the nanocomposite surface morphology study, as well as gas sensor characteristics, are shown in this section, but the performances of PG and DMF sensors are separately considered. Also, the dependence of electrical resistance of the sensors on operating temperature, as well as values of responses, response and recovery times of the sensors at various operating temperatures or target gas concentrations are shown here too.

A. Material characterization

The morphologies of the prepared SnO_2/MWCNT nanocomposite powders wit diverse compounds were studied by scanning electron microscopy using Hitachi S-4700 Type II FE-SEM equipped with a cold field emission gun operating in the range of 5–15kV. The presence of an oxide layer was confirmed by SEM-EDX. Furthermore, the crystalline structure of the inorganic layer was also studied by an X-ray diffraction method using the Rigaku Miniflex II diffractometer (angle range: 2θ [°]=10–80 utilizing characteristic X-ray (CuKα) radiation). Results of these investigations were presented in [10] [23] more detailed. Here, we are only noting that average crystalline size of SnO_2 nanoparticles estimated from SEM images and XRD patterns are less than 12 nm but the average diameter of non-covered by SnO_2 nanoparticles CNTs was about 40 nm.

B. Gas sensing characteristics

Gas sensing properties of the MWCNTs/SnO_2 nanocomposite structures were measured by home-made developed and computer-controlled static gas sensor test system [20]. The sensors were reheated and studied at different operating temperatures. When the electrical resistance of all studied sensors was stable, the vital assigned amount of compound in the liquid state for sensors testing was injected by a microsyringe in.measurement chamber Moreover, the target matters were introduced into the chamber on the special hot plate designed for the quick conversion of the liquid substance to its gas phase. After its resistance reached a new constant value, the test chamber was opened to recover the sensors in air. The sensing characteristics were studied in the 20-300°C operating temperature range and the gas response of the sensors determines as R_a/R_g where R_a and R_g are the electrical resistances in the air and in target gas-air atmosphere, respectively. The response and recovery times are determined as the time required for reaching the 90% resistance changes from the corresponding steady-state value of each signal.

C. PG vapor sensor characteristics

Firstly, we should determine the operating temperature of the sensors. As a result of measurements of the sensor resistance in air and air/gas environment, the maximal response to 650 ppm PG vapor was revealed at 200°C operating temperature (Figure 1 and Figure 2).

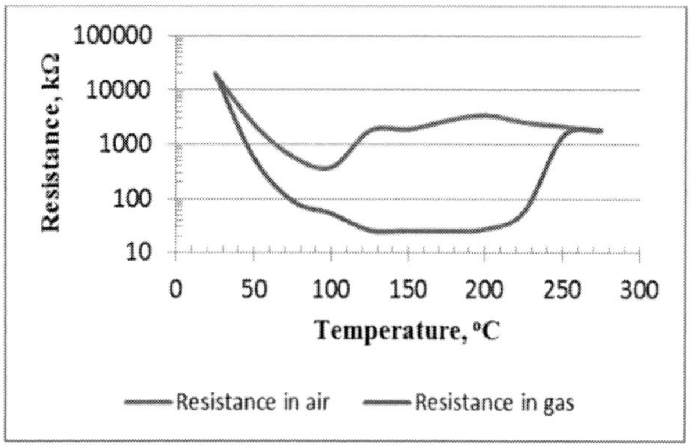

Figure 1. Dependence of electrical resistance change of MWCNTs/SnO_2 thick-film sensors on operating temperature.

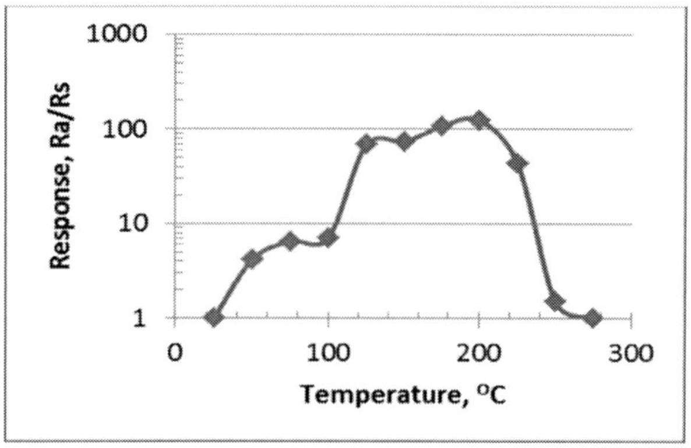

Figure 2. Response of MWCNTs/SnO_2 thick-film PG sensors vs operating temperature.

Good repeatability of the sensor response can be seen from Figure 3, where the electrical resistance change of PG sensor vs. time measured upon cyclic exposure of 650 ppm PG vapors in air at 200°C operating temperature is presented.

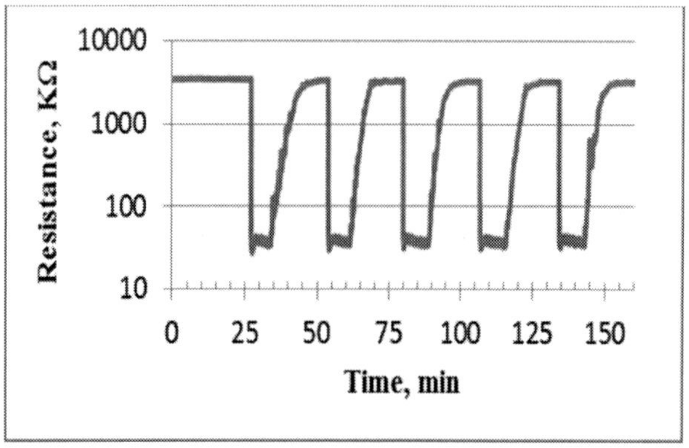

Figure 3. The electrical resistance change of MWCNTs/SnO_2 thick-film PG sensors vs time measured upon cyclic exposure of 650 ppm PG vapors in air at 200°C operating temperature.

Changes of the response of PG vapor sensor, as well as the response and recovery times depending on operating temperature, are shown in Table I. Pursuant to the Table I, maximal response to PG vapor (R_a/R_g=125) was fixed for about 5s at 200°C operating temperature, but recovery process takes place sufficiently slowly at this temperature. At higher operating temperatures, the recovery of the sensor parameters occurs for a considerably short time, but the response of the sensor decreases noticeably.

TABLE I. CHANGES OF THE 650 PPM PG VAPOR SENSOR RESPONSE AND RESPONSE AND RECOVERY TIMES AT DIFFERENT OPERATING TEMPERATURES.

Operating temperature,°C	Response, R_a/R_g	Response time,s	Recovery time, min
75	6.56	1300	100
100	7	159.6	56
125	6.2	28.8	45
150	37.8	9	11.6
175	107.1	6	21
200	125	170	10
225	43.7	6	0.83
250	1.5	3.96	0.1

Dependence of the resistance and response of MWCNTs/SnO_2 sensor on PG vapor concentration is shown in Figure 4 and Figure 5, respectively. As it is obvious from the figures, the sensor response occurs down to small target gas concentrations (15 ppm) but the response approximately linearly depends on the gas concentration.

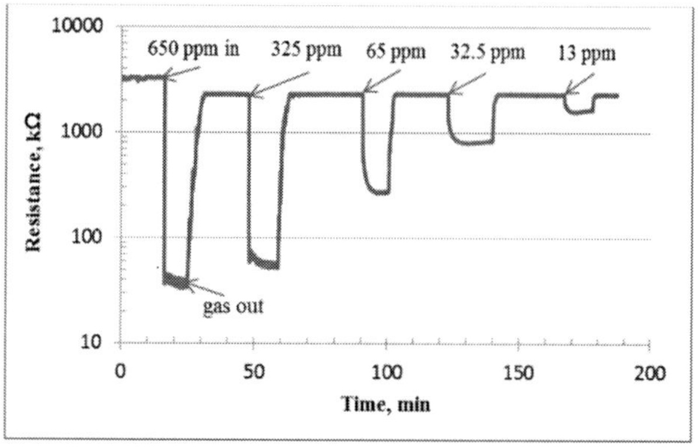

Figure 4. The response/recovery curves observed at different PG concentrations exposure measured at 200°C operating temperature.

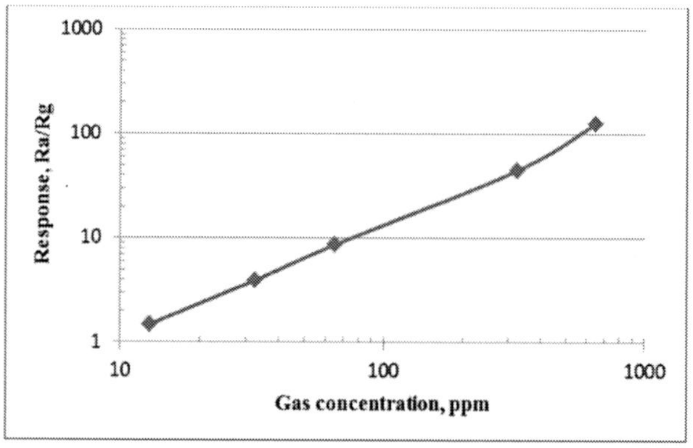

Figure 5. Dependence of the response of MWCNTs/SnO_2 PG vapor sensor on gas concentration measured at 200°C operating temperature.

D. DMF vapor sensor characteristics

The sensor response derived as a result of 500 ppm DMF vapor exposure versus operating temperature is presented in Figure 6. It can be seen that maximal response, in this case, is registered in the range of 210-225°C. Taking into account, a relatively high response, shorter response and also recovery times (see Table II), are demonstrated at 225°C operating temperature.

Dependence of the sensor response on versus DMF vapor concentration is also linear (Figure 7).

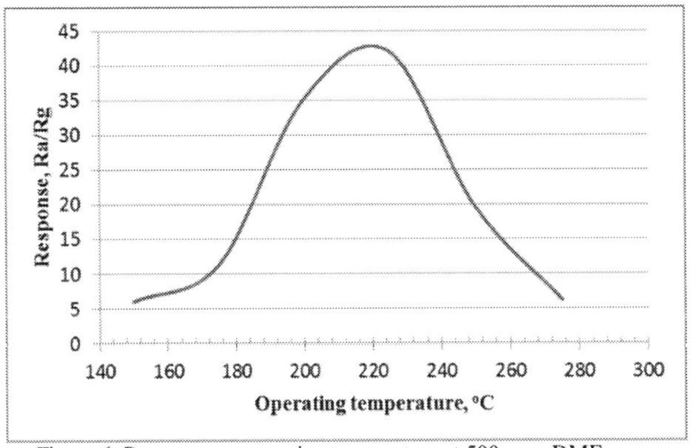

Figure 6. Response vs operating temperature at 500 ppm DMF vapor exposure.

TABLE II. CHANGES OF THE 500 PPM DMF VAPOR SENSOR RESPONSE AND RESPONSE AND RECOVERY TIMES AT DIFFERENT OPERATING TEMPERATURES.

Operating Temperature, °C	Response, Ra/Rg	Response time, s	Recovery time, s
150	6.03	90	330
175	11.42	12	240
200	35.2	6	210
225	42.04	5	50
250	19.6	4	6
275	6.2	4	1

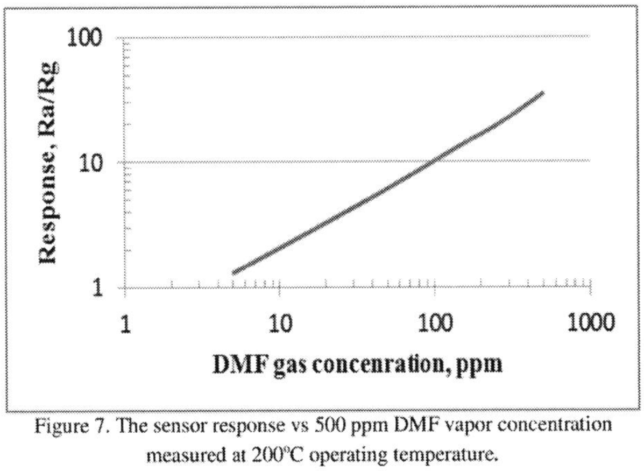

Figure 7. The sensor response vs 500 ppm DMF vapor concentration measured at 200°C operating temperature.

E. On possible mechanism of gas sensitivity

It is known that the attachment of carboxyl groups on the surface of MWCNTs is effective in nucleation and trapping the other materials including tin oxide nanoparticles. As it was shown earlier, COOH groups attached on the surface of MWCNTs have a strong interaction with alcohol vapors resulting hydrogen bond between COOH groups and the OH groups of alcohol molecules [10] [15]. This hydrogen bond should be removed by increasing the temperature, which contributes to long recovery times in MWCNTs/SnO_2 sensors.

The higher operating temperature of the gas response is observed until it reaches its maximal value. With the subsequent increase in operating temperature, desorption of chemisorbed oxygen ions takes place and gas response decreases; the recovery time decreases, too.

MWCNTs nanochannels play a smaller role at relatively more content of SnO_2 in the nanocomposite (as in our case), as nanotubes are closed by plenty of SnO_2 nanoparticles. Due to it, accessibility of gas molecules penetration to MWCNTs nanochannels through the metal-oxide thick film is very difficult. Therefore, the gas response is mainly determined by a number of metal-oxide nanoparticles and a considerable amount of surface adsorption sites. MWCNTs only prevent the formation of agglomerates of SnO_2 and ensure the development of the surface because of repulsive forces between the carboxyl groups adsorbed on it.

The oxidation reaction of PG and DMF vapors on the nanocomposite surface could be represented as follows, respectively:

$$C_3H_8O_2(g) + 8O^- \rightarrow 3CO_2(g) + 4H_2O(g) + 8e^-$$

and

$$4C_3H_7NO(g) + 42O^- \rightarrow 12CO_2(g) + 4NO_2(g) + 14H_2O(g) + 42e^-$$

At the temperature corresponding to the highest response, the reactivity of the target gas molecules is proportional to the speed of diffusion into the sensing layer. Hence, the target gas has the chance to sufficiently penetrate into the sensing layer and react with an appropriate speed. The competition between the amount of adsorbed target gases and their oxidation rate supports the maximum response and its sharp decline. With the following increase in operating temperature, desorption of the adsorbed oxygen ions from the surface of the sensor is increased. It follows that less amount of oxygen ions presents on the surface of SnO_2, might take part in reaction with target gases at higher operating temperature. Therefore, the response falls at high operating temperatures. Furthermore, it influences the physical properties of the semiconducting sensor material. For instance, at higher temperatures the carrier concentration increases (resulting from the release of electrons back to the conduction band in consequence of desorption of adsorbed oxygen) and the Debye length decreases. This may also be one of the possible reasons for the rise in R_g curve in Figure 1, which leads to the decrease in response at higher temperatures.

Although molecular weights of both considered target gases are close to each other, the quantity of carbon atoms is the same. Nevertheless, the response from DMF vapors influences less due to many adsorbed oxygen ions, resulted from the chemical decomposition, which demands for the full oxidation reaction. Thus, the 1:200 weight ratios of the nanocomposite sensor components with relatively large amount of SnO_2 particles promote an initiation of a sufficiently large quantity of ionized adsorption centers, which ensure relatively high response to DMF gas exposure.

As for selectivity, this nanocomposite sensor demonstrates cross-sensitivity to some alcohols, such as butanol, methanol and ethanol at 200°C operating temperature. Moreover, it influences by other gases, and as a rule, does not facilitate the formation of noticeable gas response at 200°C operation temperature. A sufficiently large signal is possible to obtain at higher operating temperatures, at which developed sensor does not react to diverse impacts of PG and DMF gases. For instance, the sensor exhibits a high response to toluene vapor only around of 250°C operating temperature [14] [23].

Unlike existing other type PG and DMF sensors, presented nanocomposite sensor is able to measure the concentration of mentioned gases in the atmosphere.

IV. CONCLUSION

In this paper, we have carried out the investigation of obtaining ruthenated MWCNTs/SnO_2 thick-film nanocomposite sensors using hydrothermal synthesis and sol-gel technologies. It is revealed that studied sensors give a sufficiently high response to such harmful and hazardous gases as PG and DMF at relatively low operating temperatures. The fast response of the sensors (at the order of seconds) and acceptable recovery times are observed under all gas concentrations influence at 200°C operating temperature. The minimal PG and DMF gas concentrations at which the perceptible signal is registered are 13 ppm and 5 ppm, respectively.

Due to the linear dependence of the response on the concentration of target gas, it is possible to easily measure the concentration of mentioned gases in the atmosphere.

ACKNOWLEDGMENT

This work was supported by NATO EAP SFPP 984.597.

REFERENCES

[1] G. Malaguarnera et al. "Toxic hepatitis in occupational exposure to solvents", World J. Gastroenterol. Vol. 18(22), pp. 2756–2766, 2012; doi: 10.3748/wjg.v18.i22.2756v

[2] H. Y. Chang, T. S. Shih, Y. L. Guo, C. Y. Tsai, and P. C. Hsu, "Sperm function in workers exposed to N,N-dimethylformamide in the synthetic leather industry", Fertil Steril. Vol. 81(6), pp. 1589-1594, 2004. DOI: 10.1016/j.fertnstert.2003.10.033

[3] A. Fiorito, F. Larese, S. Molinari, and T. Zanin, "Liver function alterations in synthetic leather workers exposed to dimethylformamide", American journal of industrial medicine vol. 32, pp. 255-260, 1997.

[4] V. M. Aroutiounian, "Use of Metaloxide, porous silicon and carbon nanotube gas sensors for safety and security, in Advanced Sensors for Safety and Security", A. Vaseashta, S. Khudaverdyan, eds., NATO Science for Peace and Security, Series B: Physics and Biophysics, Chapter 9, 2012.

[5] G. F. Fine, L. M. Cavanagh, A. Afonja, and R. Binions, "Metal oxide semi-conductor gas sensors in environmental monitoring", Sensors v. 10, pp. 5469-5502, 2010; doi:10.3390/s100605469.

[6] G. Korotcenkov, S. H. Han, and B. K. Cho, "Material design for metal oxide chemiresistive gas sensors", J. of Sensor Science and Technology, vol. 22, pp. 1-17, 2013: http:/dx.doi.org/10.5369/JSST.2013.22.1.1.

[7] V. M. Aroutiounian, "Gas sensors based on functionalized carbon nanotubes", Journal of Contemporary Physics (Armenian Academy of Sciences), vol. 50, pp. 333–354, 2015; Izvestiya NAN Armenii, Fizika, vol. 50, pp. 448–475, 2015; DOI: 10.3103/S1068337215040064

[8] M. M. Arafat, B. Dinan, S. A. Akbar, and A. S. M. A. Haseeb, "Gas sensors based on one dimensional nanostructured metal-oxides: A Review", Sensors, vol. 12, pp. 7207-7258, 2012; doi:10.3390/s120607207.

[9] G. Korotcenkov, S.-D. Han, B. K. Cho, and V. Brinzari, "Grain size effects in sensor response of nanostructured SnO_2- and In_2O_3-based conductometric thin film gas sensor", Critical Reviews in Solid State and Materials Sciences vol. 34, pp. 1–17, 2009; doi: 10.1080/10408430902815725.

[10] V. M. Aroutiounian et al. "Study of the surface-ruthenated SnO_2/MWCNTs nanocomposite thick-film gas sensors", Sensors and Actuators B vol. 177, pp. 308–315, 2013; doi: org/10.1016/j.snb.2012.10.106.

[11] S. A.-Feyzabad, A. A. Khodadadia, M. V.-Naseh, and Y. Mortazavi, "Highly sensitive and selective sensors to volatile organic compounds using MWCNTs/SnO_2", Sensors and Actuators B vol. 166–167, pp. 150–155, 2012; doi: 10.1016/j.snb.2012.02.024.

[12] N. V. Hieu, L. T. B. Thuy, and N. D. Chien, "Highly sensitive thin film NH_3 gas sensor operating at room temperature based on SnO_2/MWCNTs composite", Sensors and Actuators B vol. 129 pp. 888–895, 2008; doi:10.1016/j.snb.2007.09.088.

[13] X. Bai, H. Ji, P. Gao, Y. Zhang, and X. Sun, "Morphology, phase structure and acetone sensitive properties of copper-doped tungsten oxide sensors", Sens. Actuators B vol. 193, pp. 100–106, 2014; doi: org/10.1016/j.snb.2013.11.059.

[14] V. M. Aroutiounian, Z. N. Adamyan, A. G. Sayunts, E. A. Khachaturyan, and A. Z. Adamyan, "Study of MWCNT/SnO_2 nanocomposite acetone and toluene vapor sensors", Proc, of 17 Int. Conf. on Sensors and Measurement Technology, SENSOR 2015, May 19-21, Nierenberg, Germany, pp. 836-841, 2015. DOI 10.5162/sensor2015/P8.3.

[15] Z. N. Adamyan, A. G. Sayunts, E. A. Khachaturyan, and V. M. Aroutiounian, "Study of nanocomposite thick-film butanol vapor sensors",; Journal of Contemporary Physics (Armenian Academy of Sciences), vol. 51(2), pp. 143-149, 2016 Izvestiya NAN Armenii, Fizika, vol. 51, pp. 448–475, 2015; DOI: 10.3103/S1068337216020067;.

[16] V. M. Aroutiounian, "Metal oxide hydrogen, oxygen, and carbon monoxide sensors for hydrogen setups and cells", Int. J. of Hydrogen Energy vol. 32(9), pp. 1145–1158, 2007.

[17] P. Shankar, J. Bosco, and B. Rayappan, "Gas sensing mechanism of metal oxides: The role of ambient atmosphere, type of semiconductor and gases - A review", Sci. Lett., vol. 4: 126, pp. 1-18, 2015.

[18] C. Xu, J. Tamaki, N. Miura, and N. Yamazoe, "Grain size effects on gas sensitivity of porous SnO_2-based elements", Sensors and Actuators B vol. 3 pp. 147–155, 1991.

[19] A. Z. Adamyan, Z. N. Adamyan, and V. M. Aroutiounian, "Preparation of SnO_2 films with thermally stable nanoparticles", Sensors vol. 3, pp. 438–442, 2003.

[20] A. Z. Adamyan, Z. N. Adamyan, V. M. Aroutiounian, and A. H. Arakelyan, J. Turner, K. Touryan, "Sol–gel derived thin-

film semiconductor hydrogen gas sensor", Int. J. of Hydrogen Energy vol. 32, pp. 4101–4108, 2007.

[21] E. Couteau et al. "CVD synthesis of high-purity multiwalled carbon nanotubes using $CaCO_3$ catalyst support for large-scale production," Chem. Phys. Lett., vol. 378, pp. 9-17, 2003.

[22] A. Magrez, J. W. Seo, R. Smajda, M. Mionić, and L. Forró, "Catalytic CVD Synthesis of Carbon Nanotubes: Towards High Yield and Low Temperature Growth," Materials vol. 3 pp. 4871-4891, 2010.

[23] V. M. Aroutiounian et al. "Comparative study of VOC sensors based on ruthenated MWCNT/SnO_2 nanocomposites", Int. J. of Emerging Trends in Science and Technology (IJETST), vol. 01/08, pp. 1309-1319, 2014: DOI :10.18535/ijetst.

Ab Initio Investigation of CO Gas Sensing Mechanism on SnO_2 Surfaces

H.A. Zakaryan, V. M. Aroutiounian
Department of Physics of Semiconductors and Microelectronics
Yerevan State University
Yerevan, Republic of Armenia
email: zhayk91@gmail.com
email: aroutiounv1@yahoo.com

***Abstract*—This research is devoted to the investigation of the toxic CO gas adsorption mechanisms on the tin dioxide (SnO_2) semiconductor. We used density functional theory (DFT) to describe adsorption processes and found out that the Mars-van Krevelen (MvK) adsorption mechanism is not responsible for adsorption on (101) and (001) surface orientations of SnO_2, unlike for (110), (100), where CO_2 molecule forms and desorbs from the surfaces. Electronic density of states (eDoS) calculation and Bader charge analysis were done to explain the increase of surface conductance.**

Keywords-gas; sensor; DFT; CO; adsorption; Mars-van Krevelen.

I. INTRODUCTION

Carbon monoxide (CO) is tasteless and transparent substance, which is known as an "invisible killer" due to the high level of toxicity. It is extremely poisonous and can even cause health effects up to a certain extent - 9ppm, therefore, the detection of CO in the environment is quite vital. For the above reasons, chemical sensors are used to precisely monitor the concentration of the target compounds in the air. Usually, the SnO_2 semiconductor is used as a sensing material in such detectors, because of high sensitivity and low response time for wide variety of molecules, such as CO, H_2, CH_3OH, NO_x, etc. [1]–[8]. In order to increase the sensitivity of the detectors, it is crucial to deeply investigate adsorption mechanism of CO compounds.

Several models, which are named as Langmuir Hishelwood [9][10], Eley Redeal [11] and the MvK [12], have been developed to describe the mechanisms that are responsible for CO adsorption on oxide semiconductors. The MvK adsorbtion mechanism is in a good agreement with the experiments on SnO_2–(110) surface [13][14]. Apparently, the MvK mechanism consists of following steps; *I)* adsorbed CO molecule is reacting with tin dioxide oxygen and forms CO_2 compound, leaving oxygen vacancy in the material; *II)* then remained vacancy fills by adsorbed O_2 molecule from the environment; *III)* and finally, another CO molecule is reacting with already bonded O_2 and forms CO_2, leaving material in its initial undisturbed state.

We would like to stress that there are plenty of manuscripts dedicated to the investigation of CO absorption on SnO_2 surfaces, using first principle and ab initio DFT calculations [15][16]. Some calculations were done particularly for pristine (110) surface orientation [17], oxygen reach [18] and tainted surfaces [19]. However, very few are devoted to other surface orientations (100), (101) [5] and (001) [6]. In practice, surface orientation immensely influences sensor parameters such as sensitivity, time response etc.

In this manuscript, we explore CO adsorption on various surface orientations (110), (100), (101), (001) of SnO_2 and determine the most optimal configurations for adsorption, using ab initio DFT calculations in order to shed the light on the atomic scale processes that still remains elusive and unclear. Here, we will rise following issues: *I)* Does MvK mechanism similarly describing adsorption processes for all surface orientations of SnO_2? *II)* What is the exact amount of charge transferred between the surface and adsorbed CO molecule? *III)* Which surface orientation is more prominent to the interaction with the CO molecule?

The paper is organized in the following way: Section *II)* is devoted to computational methods and surface/bulk structure of SnO_2 sensing material. Section *III)* is devoted to the adsorption processes, eDoS calculations for the various surface orientations of SnO_2. Section *IV)* is dedicated to discussions and conclusions.

II. MODELS AND COMPUTATIONAL METHODS

Calculations were done using conventional ab initio DFT [20][21] method implemented in Vienna ab initio Simulation Package (VASP) [22]–[24]. DFT relaxations were done within Perdew-Burke-Ernzerhof (PBE) generalized gradient approximation (GGA) [25]. The 500eV cutoff energy was chosen due to the total energy convergence from that value. Surface structures were relaxed until the threshold net force on atoms become less than 0.01 eV/A. The Monkhorst-Pack scheme [26] was used to sample the Brillouin zone, using 6x6x1 k-points mesh. After relaxation, the

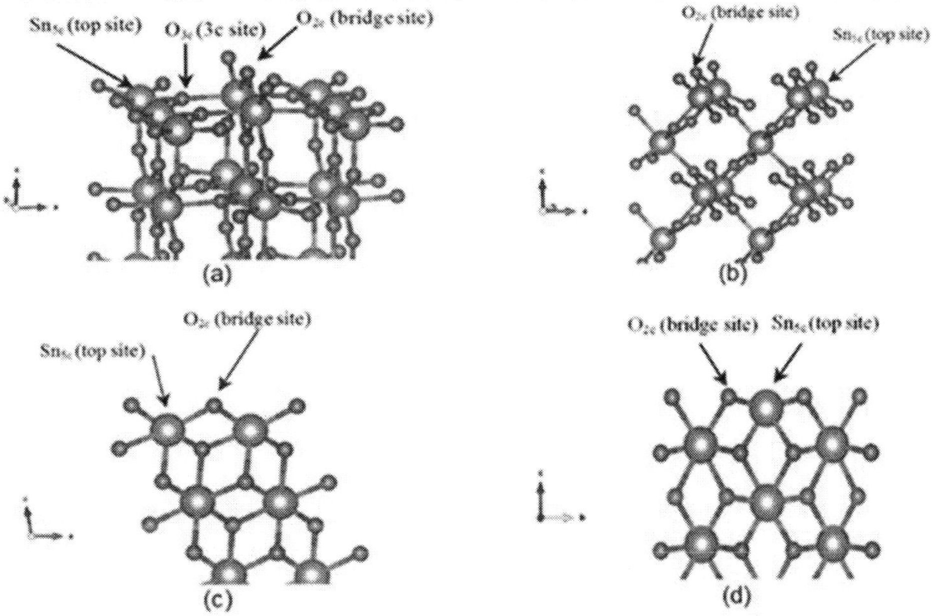

Figure 1. Different surfaces of SnO_2 and possible adsorption sites on it. a) (110) b) (100) c) (101) d) (001)

Bader charge analysis was done to find out charge transfer [27]–[29].

Stable adsorbed configurations were found using the following equation:

$$E_{ads}=E_{surf}-E_{clean}-E_{CO}\,, \quad (1)$$

where E_{ads} is adsorption energy, E_{surf} is total energy of SnO_2 surface and adsorbed CO, E_{clean} is total energy of pure surface without CO and E_{CO} is total energy of the gas molecule. It is clear from this equation that if E_{ads} is negative the configuration of adsorbed site is stable, in other words, the process is exothermic. In the case of positive E_{ads}, the process is endothermic: the molecule will not adsorb to the surface and will remain in the non-interacting state.

Bulk SnO_2 has rutile, tetragonal structure, corresponding to the $P4_2/mnm$ space group. The lattice parameters of SnO2 from [30]–[32] are a = 4.82 Å, c = 3.23 Å and u = 0.607. In our calculations (see Fig. 1) each (110), (100), (101), (001) surface consists of 4 layers and relative stability has the following sequence (110), (100), (101), (001) [6]. Here, number of layers was tuned to check the convergence of surface energy. However, after getting all results, we double checked the obtained data by recalculating stable structures with a big substrate of 12 atoms of tin and 24 atoms of oxygen and make sure that the results are reliable. For all calculations, we choose vacuum thickness of 15 Å, which is greater than substrate thickness. For each surface, the electronic density of states (eDoS) was calculated and established that the gap between valence and conduction bands was underestimated, because of the self-consistency of DFT calculations. From experiments, it is known that value of band gap is 3.6 eV, but we get 1 eV, which is in accordance with previous DFT calculations [33].

III. RESULTS AND DISCUSSION

In this section, each surface orientation would be described separately. Bader charge analysis, eDoS and stable structures would be presented as well.

A. SnO_2 (110) surface

This surface orientation consists of 4 layers, each comprising of 3 subsequent layers. Top sublayer represents oxygen, where each atom (O_{2c}) is connected by the covalent bond to 2 Sn atoms. The Second sublayer has 2 Sn atoms and 2 oxygen atoms. Third one is similar to the first layer. So, together these 3 sublayers can be treated as one layer which is continually repeated 4 times (see Fig1 a). There are 3 possible adsorption sites: top site (t), bridge site (br), three-coordinated oxygen site (3c). For each site, we consider 2 configurations: *I)* C atom in a CO molecule is closer to the surface (C down configuration) and *II)* the vice versa configuration (O down configuration). Thus, we end up with 6 possible configurations for (110) surface.

For each separate configuration calculated adsorption energies are given in Table I. As we can clearly see the O down configuration for all surfaces is completely unstable.

In the case of C down configuration, (110) surface has 3 stable sites. However, there is only one that is transferring the charge form molecule to the surface, and it is corresponding to the event when molecule approaches to br-site, reacts with oxygen and takes it away forming a CO_2 molecule and leaves oxygen vacancy on the surface. Here, vacancy could be an adsorption site for O_2 or CO molecule, as described in [15][18]. The eDoS of surface reveals that conductivity of the surface increases by decreasing of the band gap. The Bader charge analysis shows charge transport to the surface of 1.7e. Such processes examined in a number of experimental and theoretical studies [13][15][18]. It is important to note, that for this particular configuration and surface orientation the first step of MvK mechanism is preserved, and the distance between CO_2 molecule and surface is 3.1 Å.

For other sites (top and 3c) the CO molecule does not exchange electrons, which serves as a confirmation that we have physisorption process onto the surface. In these cases, band gap does not change and distances from carbon to tin atoms are 2.46, 2.61 Å, respectively.

TABLE I. ADSORPTION ENERGIES, DISTANCES AND BADER CHARGE ANALYSIS OF (110) SURFACE.

Ads. sites and configurations	Values of E_{ads}, distance and bader charge		
	E_{ads}(eV)	*CO distanced surface(Å)*	*Charge transferred to surface(e)*
br	-0.48	3.1	1.7
br(O down)	0.31	2.58	0.0
top	-0.16	2.465	0.0
top(O down)	0.01	2.69	0.0
3c	-0.03	2.61	0.0
3c(O down)	0.5	2.62	0.0

B. SnO_2 (100) surface

For (100) surface orientation the unit cell also consists of same 4 layers, where each layer can be divided into 3 sublayers: O-Sn-O layers. The top atom of the surface is 2 coordinated oxygen as in (110) surface, see Fig. 1 b. Adsorption energies for possible two site configurations are given in Table II. According to the calculations interaction of CO with the O_{2c} site of oxygen leads to the formation of CO_2 molecule and also leaves a vacancy on the surface (Fig. 2 a).

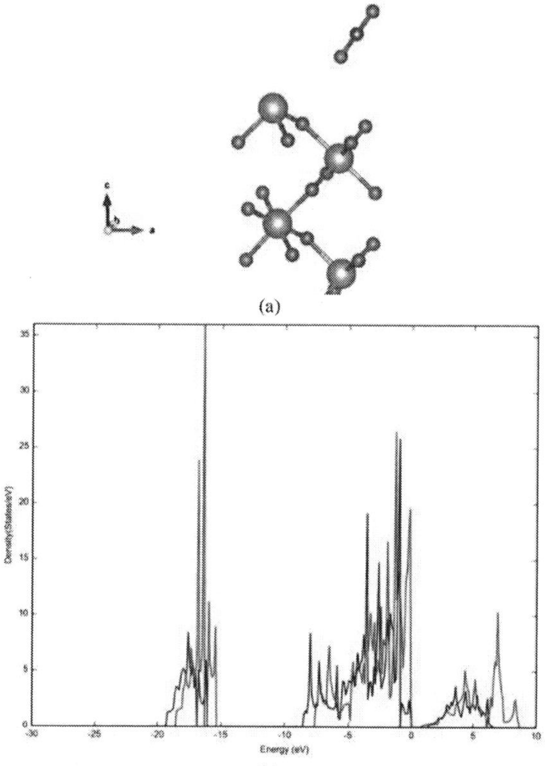

Figure 2. Structure and eDoS of (100) surface. a) Desorbed CO_2 molecule from (100) surface (red circle is oxygen, grey is Sn, brown is C atoms). b) eDoS of substrate before adsorption (red line), and after CO_2 desorption. (blue line).

TABLE II. ADSORPTION ENERGIES, DISTANCES AND BADER CHARGE ANALYSIS OF (100) SURFACE.

Ads. sites	Values of E_{ads}, distance and bader charge		
	E_{ads}(eV)	*CO distanced surface(Å)*	*Charge transferred to surface(e)*
br	-0.48	3.25	1.6
top	-0.16	2.65	0.0

In this case, the first step of MvK mechanism is also conserved and it leads to charge transfer of 1.6e to the surface. Therefore, the surface conductance is increasing, because of transferred charge leading to the band gap reduction by 0.1eV in comparison to the uncharged surface, see Fig. 2 b. Here, the blue lines represent the eDoS after desorption that correspond to 3.25 Å distance from CO molecule to surface.

The Second possible adsorption site is top(t) on Sn atom. Here as for (110), the CO is physisorbed and no charge transfer has been observed. Due to physisorption, the distance from a carbon atom of CO molecule to the oxygen atom of the surface is 2.65 Å.

C. SnO_2 (101) surface

In the case of (101) surface orientation, each of 4 layers consists of 3 subsequent layers of 2O, 2Sn, 2O. There are 3 possible sites of adsorptions O_{2c}, Sn atom and 3 coordinated O, which is located in third sub layer as it is shown in Fig. 1 (c). Here, only one configuration has negative adsorption energy and it is O_{2c} (TABLE III).

TABLE III. ADSORPTION ENERGIES, DISTANCES AND BADER CHARGE ANALYSIS OF (101) SURFACE.

Ads. sites	**Values of E_{ads}, distance and bader charge**		
	E_{ads}(eV)	***CO distanced surface(Å)***	***Charge transferred to surface(e)***
O_{2c}	-0.47	1.18	1.9

The CO molecule adsorbs by the surface and remains connected to it in O_{2c} site with a distance of 1.18 Å (see Fig. 3). During that process, the distance between O_{2c} oxygen and Sn atom increases up to 2.5 Å. The Bader charge analysis shows that there is 1.9e charge transferred to the surface, which make it more conductive. Thus, adsorption mechanism on (101) surface differs from MvK, because no CO_2 desorption observed. Conductivity increases and band gap decreases due to transferred charge, see Fig. 3 (b), where blue lines represent eDoS after adsorption and have more states around Fermi level (Energy = 0 in the horizontal axis).

D. SnO_2 (001) surface

In this case, we have a completely different situation. Instead of 4 layers that consist of 3 subsequent layers, we have got only one that consists of one atom of Sn and 2 oxygen atoms. There are two possible sites: on top of Sn (t) site and O_{2c} (2c) site Fig. 1 (d). Moreover, there are 2 equivalent 2c sites in one unit cell, thus we should take into account two possible coverages. The first is when both sites are occupied by the CO molecule and form one mono layer (ML=1). The second possible coverage is when only one site is occupied and half mono layer of CO forms (ML = 0.5). For ML = 0.5, carbon monoxide adsorbed and stay bounded with a distance of 1.16 Å (Fig. 4) to the O_{2c} atom, transferring 2e charge to the substrate (see TABLE IV).

For ML = 1, one CO molecule adsorbed and one physisorbed in a 1.255 and 2.6 Å distances, respectively. In fact, for (001) only ML=0.5 coverage can happen, because when one CO adsorbed, the second one will be physisorbed. Bader charge analysis shows that 1.83e was transferred to the surface.

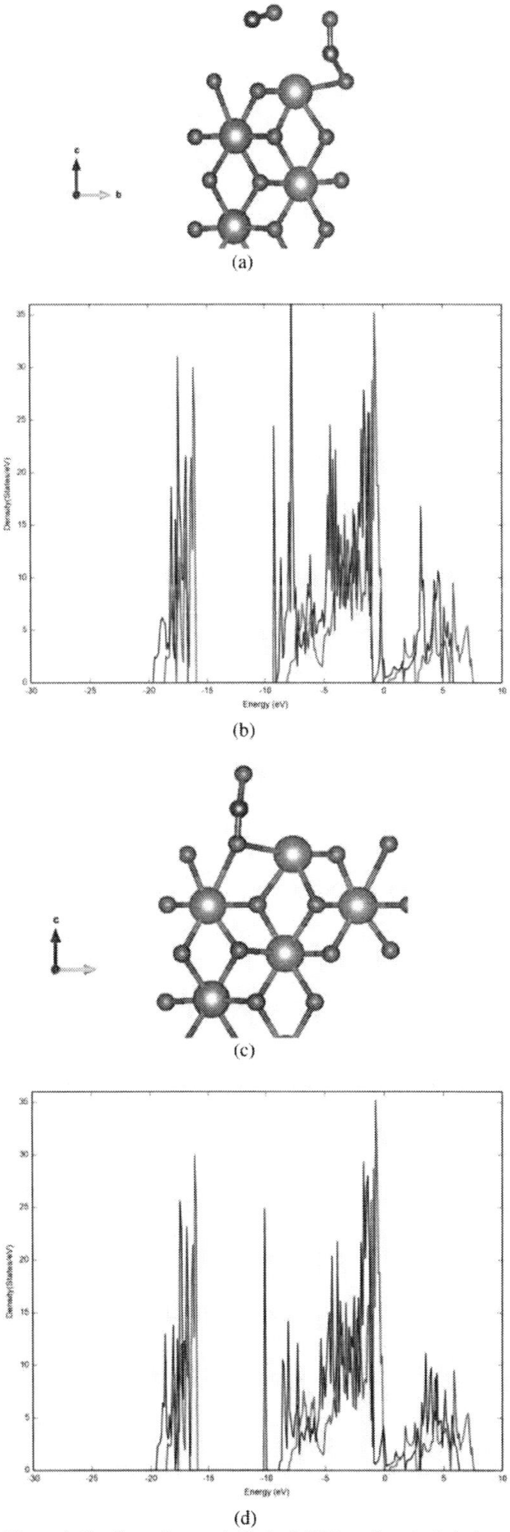

Figure 4. Configurations and eDoS of (001) surface (red circle is oxygen, grey is Sn, brown is C atoms). (a) Adsorption when ML=1.(b) eDoS before and after adsorption, when ML = 1 (b) Adsorption when ML= 0.5 (d)) eDoS before and after adsorption, when ML = 1.

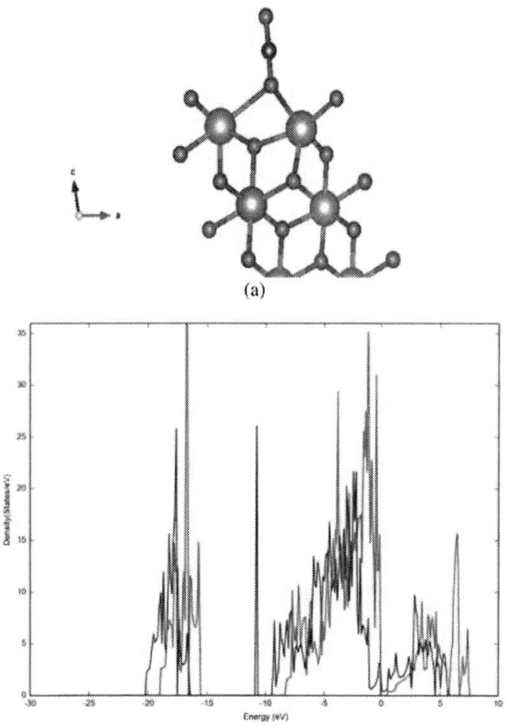

(a)

(b)

Figure 3.a) Adsorbed CO on (101) surface (red circle is oxygen, grey is Sn, brown is C atoms). b) eDoS of clean (101) surface (red line) and CO adsorbed on it (blue line).

TABLE IV. ADSORPTION ENERGIES, DISTANCES AND BADER CHARGE ANALYSIS OF (001) SURFACE.

Adsorption sites	Values of E_{ads}, distance and bader charge		
	E_{ads}(eV)	*CO distanced surface(Å)*	*Charge transferred to surface(e)*
2c, ML = 0.5	-1.19	1.16	2.0
2c, ML = 1	-1.24	1.25	1.8
top	-0.19	2.41	0.0

In both cases, surface conduction increases and band gap decreases due to charge transfer from the CO molecule. On Fig. 4 (b)(d), the red lines represent eDoS of undistorted surface and blue correspond to the eDoS after adsorption, which has more states around Fermi level compared to undistorted surfaces eDoS. Physisorption occurs for the top site with distance 2.41 Å.

IV. Conclusion

Previously, it was considered that adsorption on SnO_2 surfaces follows MvK mechanism; however, here we have proven that CO adsorption on SnO2(101), (001) is different. Here, the C atom of the CO molecule remains bonded to surface's O atom. Also, we find out that in the case of (001) surface orientation CO coverage can be only half mono layer (ML = 0.5). For (110) and (100) surfaces, we establish that adsorption obeys MvK mechanism, where its first stage CO_2 molecules are forming during CO-surface interaction. For all adsorption cases, O down configuration was not stable, due to positive adsorption energy.

The Bader charge analysis reveals that charge transfer to (101), (001) surfaces are 1.9e, 2e respectively and 1.7e, 1.6e for (110), (100) surfaces. The eDoS combined with Bader analysis shows that (101), (001) surface orientations gather more electrons than the rest orientations, thus, those should be considered as a better platform for the interaction of the CO molecules with SnO2 surfaces. We believe that our findings will pave the way for the fabrication of SnO2 based CO sensors with higher sensitivity and lower response time.

Acknowledgment

This work was supported by NATO project SfP-984597. We are grateful to Prof. Artem Oganov for opportunities to perform the DFT calculations on the Rurik supercomputer at Moscow Institute of Physics and Technology (State University). We are also thankful to Davit Ghazaryan and Dr. Alexander Kvashnin for the useful discussions and significant amendments of this manuscript.

References

[1] V. Aroutiounian, "Metal oxide hydrogen, oxygen, and carbon monoxide sensors for hydrogen setups and cells," Int. J. Hydrog. Energy, vol. 32, no. 9, Jun. 2007, pp. 1145–1158, doi:10.1016/j.ijhydene.2007.01.004.

[2] V. M. Aroutiounian, "Metal oxide gas sensors decorated with carbon nanotubes," Lith. J. Phys., vol. 55, no. 4, Dec. 2015, pp. 319–329, doi:10.3952/physics.v55i4.3230.

[3] V. M. Aroutiounian et al., "Manufacturing and investigations of i-butane sensor made of SnO2/multiwall-carbon-nanotube nanocomposite," Sens. Actuators B Chem., vol. 173, Oct. 2012, pp. 890–896, doi:10.1016/j.snb.2012.04.039.

[4] M. Batzill and U. Diebold, "The surface and materials science of tin oxide," Prog. Surf. Sci., vol. 79, no. 2–4, 2005, pp. 47–154, doi:10.1016/j.progsurf.2005.09.002.

[5] S. Gong et al., "Gas sensing characteristics of SnO2 thin films and analyses of sensor response by the gas diffusion theory," Mater. Sci. Eng. B, vol. 164, no. 2, Aug. 2009, pp. 85–90, doi:10.1016/j.mseb.2009.07.008.

[6] C. Xu, Y. Jiang, D. Yi, S. Sun, and Z. Yu, "Environment-dependent surface structures and stabilities of SnO2 from the first principles," J. Appl. Phys., vol. 111, no. 6, Feb. 2012, pp. 63504 1-9, doi:10.1063/1.3694033.

[7] A. Adamyan et.al, "Sol–gel derived thin-film semiconductor hydrogen gas sensor," Int. J. Hydrog. Energy, vol. 32, no. 16, Nov. 2007, pp. 4101–4108, doi:10.1016/j.ijhydene.2007.03.043.

[8] A. Z. Adamyan, Z. N. Adamyan, and V. M. Aroutiounian, "Study of sensitivity and response kinetics changes for SnO2 thin-film hydrogen sensors," Int. J. Hydrog. Energy, vol. 34,

no. 19, Oct. 2009, pp. 8438–8443, doi:10.1016/j.ijhydene.2009.08.001.

[9] R. H. Nibbelke, M. A. J. Campman, J. H. B. J. Hoebink, and G. B. Marin, "Kinetic Study of the CO Oxidation over Pt/γ-Al2O3and Pt/Rh/CeO2/γ-Al2O3in the Presence of H2O and CO2," J. Catal., vol. 171, no. 2, Oct. 1997, pp. 358–373, doi:10.1006/jcat.1997.1785.

[10] I. Langmuir, "The mechanism of the catalytic action of platinum in the reactions 2Co + O2= 2Co2 and 2H2+ O2= 2H2O," Trans. Faraday Soc., vol. 17, 1922, pp. 621–654, doi:10.1039/tf9221700621.

[11] C. C. Cheng, S. R. Lucas, H. Gutleben, W. J. Choyke, and J. T. Yates, "Atomic hydrogen-driven halogen extraction from silicon(100): Eley-Rideal surface kinetics," J. Am. Chem. Soc., vol. 114, no. 4, Feb. 1992, pp. 1249–1252, doi:10.1021/ja00030a020.

[12] P. Mars and D. W. van Krevelen, "Oxidations carried out by means of vanadium oxide catalysts," Chem. Eng. Sci., vol. 3, 1954, pp. 41–59, doi:10.1016/S0009-2509(54)80005-4.

[13] Y. Sun et.al, "Atomically Thin Tin Dioxide Sheets for Efficient Catalytic Oxidation of Carbon Monoxide," Angew. Chem. Int. Ed., vol. 52, no. 40, Sep. 2013, pp. 10569–10572, doi:10.1002/anie.201305530.

[14] J. Yu, D. Zhao, X. Xu, X. Wang, and N. Zhang, "Study on RuO2/SnO2: Novel and Active Catalysts for CO and CH4 Oxidation," ChemCatChem, vol. 4, no. 8, Aug. 2012, pp. 1122–1132, doi:10.1002/cctc.201200038.

[15] Z. Lu et al., "Direct CO oxidation by lattice oxygen on the SnO 2(110) surface: a DFT study," Phys Chem Chem Phys, vol. 16, no. 24, 2014, pp. 12488–12494, doi:10.1039/C4CP00540F.

[16] M. Melle-Franco and G. Pacchioni, "CO adsorption on SnO2(110): cluster and periodic ab initio calculations," Surf. Sci., vol. 461, no. 1–3, Aug. 2000, pp. 54–66, doi:10.1016/S0039-6028(00)00528-8.

[17] F. Ciriaco, L. Cassidei, M. Cacciatore, and G. Petrella, "First principle study of processes modifying the conductivity of substoichiometric SnO2 based materials upon adsorption of CO from atmosphere," Chem. Phys., vol. 303, no. 1–2, Aug. 2004, pp. 55–61, doi: 10.1016/j.chemphys.2004.05.005.

[18] X. Wang, H. Qin, Y. Chen, and J. Hu, "Sensing Mechanism of SnO2 (110) Surface to CO: Density Functional Theory Calculations," J. Phys. Chem. C, vol. 118, no. 49, Dec. 2014, pp. 28548–28561, doi:10.1021/jp501880r.

[19] Y. B. Xue and Z. A. Tang, "Density functional study of the interaction of CO with undoped and Pd doped SnO2(110) surface," Sens. Actuators B Chem., vol. 138, no. 1, Apr. 2009 pp. 108–112, doi:10.1016/j.snb.2009.02.030.

[20] P. Hohenberg and W. Kohn, "Inhomogeneous Electron Gas," Phys. Rev., vol. 136, no. 3B, Nov. 1964, pp. B864–B871, doi:10.1103/PhysRev.136.B864.

[21] W. Kohn and L. J. Sham, "Self-Consistent Equations Including Exchange and Correlation Effects," Phys. Rev., vol. 140, no. 4A, Nov. 1965, pp. A1133–A1138, doi:10.1103/PhysRev.140.A1133.

[22] G. Kresse and J. Hafner, "Ab initio molecular dynamics for liquid metals," Phys. Rev. B, vol. 47, no. 1, Jan. 1993, pp. 558–561, doi:10.1103/PhysRevB.47.558.

[23] G. Kresse and J. Hafner, "Ab initio molecular-dynamics simulation of the liquid-metal–amorphous-semiconductor transition in germanium," Phys. Rev. B, vol. 49, no. 20, May 1994, pp. 14251–14269, doi:10.1103/PhysRevB.49.14251.

[24] G. Kresse and J. Furthmüller, "Efficient iterative schemes for ab initio total-energy calculations using a plane-wave basis set," Phys. Rev. B, vol. 54, no. 16, Oct. 1996, pp. 11169–11186, doi:10.1103/PhysRevB.54.11169.

[25] J. P. Perdew, K. Burke, and M. Ernzerhof, "Generalized Gradient Approximation Made Simple," Phys. Rev. Lett., vol. 77, no. 18, Oct. 1996, pp. 3865–3868, doi:10.1103/PhysRevLett.77.3865.

[26] H. J. Monkhorst and J. D. Pack, "Special points for Brillouin-zone integrations," Phys. Rev. B, vol. 13, no. 12, Jun. 1976, pp. 5188–5192, doi:10.1103/PhysRevB.13.5188.

[27] G. Henkelman, A. Arnaldsson, and H. Jónsson, "A fast and robust algorithm for Bader decomposition of charge density," Comput. Mater. Sci., vol. 36, no. 3, Jun. 2006, pp. 354–360, doi:10.1016/j.commatsci.2005.04.010.

[28] E. Sanville, S. D. Kenny, R. Smith, and G. Henkelman, "Improved grid-based algorithm for Bader charge allocation," J. Comput. Chem., vol. 28, no. 5, Apr. 2007, pp. 899–908, doi:10.1002/jcc.20575.

[29] W. Tang, E. Sanville, and G. Henkelman, "A grid-based Bader analysis algorithm without lattice bias," J. Phys. Condens. Matter, vol. 21, no. 8, Feb. 2009, pp.84204 1-7, doi:10.1088/0953-8984/21/8/084204.

[30] T. T. Rantala, T. S. Rantala, and V. Lantto, "Surface relaxation of the (110) face of rutile SnO2," Surf. Sci., vol. 420, no. 1, Jan. 1999, pp. 103–109, doi:10.1016/S0039-6028(98)00833-4.

[31] I. Manassidis and M. j. Gillan, "First-principles study of SnO2 (110)," Surf. Rev. Lett., vol. 1, no. 4, Dec. 1994, pp. 491–494, doi10.1142/S0218625X94000503.

[32] T. T. Rantala, T. S. Rantala, and V. Lantto, "Electronic structure of SnO2 (110) surface," Mater. Sci. Semicond. Process., vol. 3, no. 1–2, Mar. 2000, pp. 103–107, doi:10.1016/S1369-8001(00)00021-4.

[33] Y. Duan, "Electronic properties and stabilities of bulk and low-index surfaces of SnO in comparison with Sn O 2 : A first-principles density functional approach with an empirical correction of van der Waals interactions," Phys. Rev. B, vol. 77, no. 4, Jan. 2008, pp. 045332 1-22 doi:10.1103/PhysRevB.77.045332.

Aluminum-doped Zinc Oxide Nanocrystals for NO_2 Detection at Low Temperature

Sandrine Bernardini [1], Bruno Lawson [1], Khalifa Aguir [1]
Aix Marseille Univ, Univ Toulon, CNRS, IM2NP, Marseille, France
e-mail: sandrine.bernardini@im2np.fr
e-mail: bruno.lawson@im2np.fr
e-mail: khalifa.aguir@im2np.fr

Olivier Margeat [2], Christine Videlot-Ackermann [2], Jörg Ackermann [2]
Aix Marseille Univ, CNRS, CINaM, Marseille, France
e-mail: olivier.margeat@univ-amu.fr
e-mail: videlot@cinam.univ-mrs.fr
e-mail: ackermann@cinam.univ-mrs.fr

***Abstract* — In this work, we focus on nitrogen dioxide (NO_2) detection at temperature up to 100°C in order to be compatible with most of flexible substrates. Such low temperatures require dedicated materials, as Zinc Oxide (ZnO), a widely used material for its sensing properties. Functionalization or doping is a growing research activity to improve sensor sensibility at lower gas concentrations and lower working temperatures. Aluminum-doped Zinc Oxide (Al-ZnO) has been shown as a possible way for NO_2 detection. Moreover, nanocrystals improve the gas detection due to their high surface/volume ratio. Therefore in this work, Al-ZnO nanocrystals have been deposited by drop coating from colloidal solution as sensitive layer for air quality monitoring. The platform consists of Ti/Pt interdigitated electrodes on Si/SiO_2 substrate. Herein, a brief description of the process steps will be provided. Gas sensing properties have been investigated in dark and under ultraviolet illumination at various heating excitation from room temperature around 25°C up to 100°C. These sensors present repeatable responses toward (NO_2) with fast responses for low gas concentrations as low as 0.2 ppm.**

Keywords-Gas sensor; NO_2 sensor; light excitation; Al-ZnO nanocrystals, Ultraviolet illumination.

I. Introduction

Nitrogen dioxide comes from vehicles, power plants, industrial emissions and off-road sources, such as construction, lawn and gardening equipment. It is one of the most dangerous air pollutants. It plays a major role in the formation of ozone and acid rain. Continued or frequent exposure to NO_2 concentrations higher than 150 ppb may cause incidence of acute respiratory. These concentrations are detectable by ZnO, a widely used material for its sensing properties [1]. Aluminum-doped Zinc Oxide (Al-ZnO) has been shown as a possible way for NO_2 detection as low as 20 ppm [2]. Moreover, Pr. Morante's team has reported that illuminating metal oxide gas sensors with ultraviolet (UV) light improve SnO_2 nanowires performances to NO_2 detection [3]. In this work, NO_2 detections have been made under UV illumination by Al-ZnO nanocrystals deposited on interdigitated electrodes fabricated on Si/SiO_2 substrate using photolithography. In Section II, the Al-ZnO solution process will be described and the results will be discussed in Section III.

II. Description of Approach and Techniques

This description is composed of two parts, one is the sensing film fabrication; the other is the measurement system set-up.

A. Al-ZnO solution

The Al-ZnO nanocrystals were obtained by a surfactant-free chemical synthesis approach using zinc acetate and aluminum isopropylate as precursors with potassium hydroxide [4]. Fig. 1 shows a typical Transmission Electron Microscopy (TEM) image of the Al-ZnO nanocrystals, evidencing their size (diameter about 10 nm) and homogeneous size and shape dispersions.

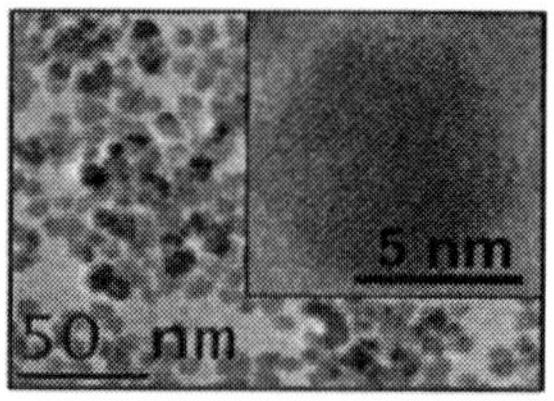

Figure 1. TEM image of AZO nanocrystals drop-casted on a TEM grid.

The Aluminum doping level of 0.8 at. % was controlled by the metal precursors ratio, and determined by inductively coupled plasma mass spectrometry (ICP-MS) analyses. The Al-ZnO nanocrystals were dispersed in isopropanol as solvent using ethanolamine as short-chain surfactant to obtain aggregate-free solution. Al-ZnO nanocrystals drop casting allows the formation of thin films with improved conductivity compared to ZnO nanocrystals reference, both with and without low temperature annealing.

B. Gas sensors

Our gas sensor consists of Ti/Pt interdigitated electrodes for gas detection. Temperature is controlled underneath up to 100°C to improve the gas detection. The metal electrodes Ti/Pt were deposited on Si/SiO_2 by magnetron sputtering with thicknesses of 5 nm and 100 nm, respectively. In this work, Al-ZnO nanocrystals were deposited by drop coating. They were used as sensitive material with a thickness of 200 nm measured by a Dektak 6M stylus profiler. The Al-ZnO films obtained were annealed for 30 min at 150°C for removing solvents and improving their quality and stability. The aim was to study the possible use, in a future work, on flexible substrates which do not allow temperature process higher than 150°C. In order to find the best operating conditions, the gas detections were carried out in a closed chamber by measuring the resistance through the sensitive material using UV light (λ = 325 nm) and temperature excitations (up to 100°C) under 30 s exposures to NO_2. We used a power supply to control the operating temperature, a SourceMeter Keithley 2450 for the data acquisition and one UV Light-Emitting Diode (LED) for UV illumination situated at 10 mm from the sensing material to obtained more photogenerated charge carriers.

III. Results and Discussion

The gas sensor fabricated with Al-ZnO nanoparticles as sensitive material and deposited by drop coating on Si/SiO_2 substrate is presented in Fig. 2.

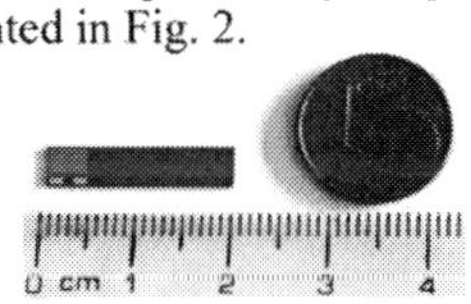

Figure 2. Sensor fabricated on Si/SiO_2 substrate.

Gas response of a gas sensor is defined by (1) as the ratio of the resistance change on the surface of the gas sensor before and after being exposed to NO_2:

$$R = R_a/R_{NO2} \quad (1)$$

where R_a is the sensor resistance through dry airflow and R_{NO2} the sensor resistance in presence of NO_2.

Detection was possible in dark at 25°C, but without coming back to the baseline (not shown here). From 75°C, the resistance returns to its reference value obtained through dry airflow. In dark, our best operating temperature has been determined at 100°C. Fig. 3 shows responses in dark for 0.2 ppm to 2 ppm of NO_2 at 100°C.

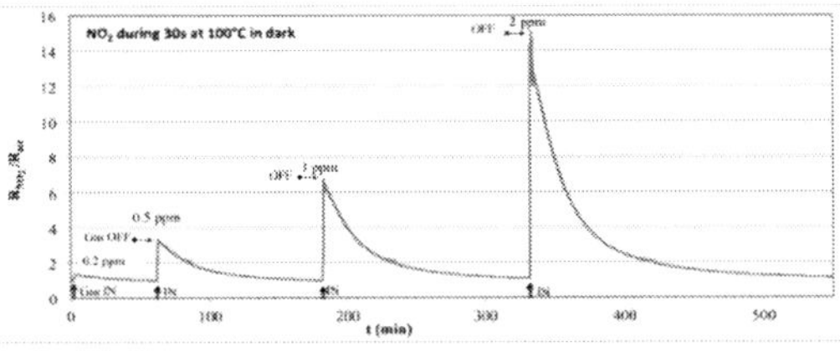

Figure 3. Sensor responses at 100°C in dark for 0.2 ppm to 2 ppm NO_2.

Oxygen vacancies on metal-oxide surfaces function as n-type donors increasing the conductivity of oxide. When Al-ZnO gets exposed to NO_2 (a typical oxidizing gas), an increase in resistance occurs due to oxygen ion adsorption from NO_2 on the surface by trapping of electrons. Under UV illumination, the interaction between NO_2 and oxide is greatly enhanced with the abundant photogenerated free electron. Similarly, UV illumination facilitates desorption of oxygen anions into neutral gaseous oxygen by providing photogenerated holes during the recovering period. Under continuous UV illumination, it was possible to detect low NO_2 concentrations at room temperature and return to the sensor resistance in dry air after stopping the gas injection. However, Fig. 4 shows that, at 25°C under UV, about 45 minutes are needed to return to the baseline.

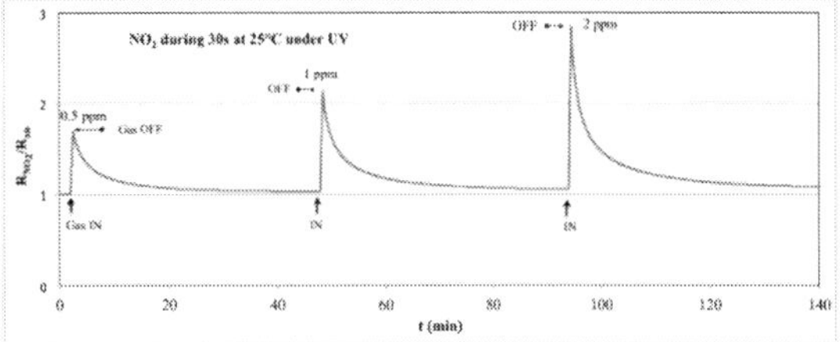

Figure 4. Sensor responses at 25°C under UV for 0.5 ppm to 2 ppm NO_2.

By increasing the temperature up to 100°C, the response amplitude is multiplied by 10 at least and the time to return to the baseline is divided by 8. Fig. 5 illustrates sensor responses at 100°C under UV light illumination for 0.2 ppm to 2 ppm of NO_2.

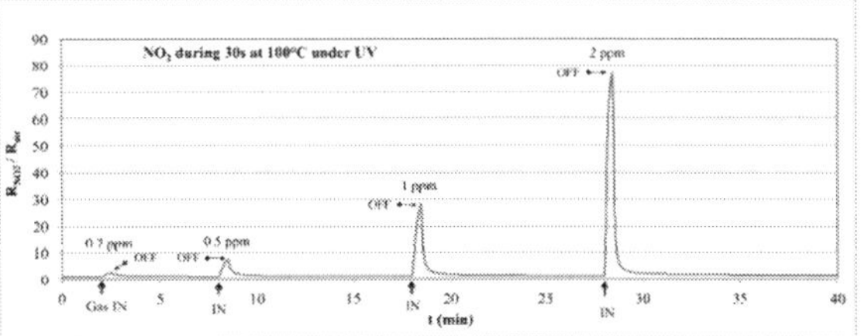

Figure 5. Sensor responses at 100°C under UV light for 0.2 to 2 ppm NO_2.

IV. Conclusion

This paper reports nitrogen dioxide (NO_2) detection at temperature up to 100°C. Room temperature NO_2 detection have been achieved by sensors on rigid substrate and improved with one UV LED illumination. The gas measurements in our experiments under UV showed good responses with fast response / return times towards NO_2 even at 0.2 ppm. The photogenerated charge carriers (electrons and holes) present important benefits for working at low temperatures. UV light illumination results in an increase in the response signal, enhanced sensing reversibility, and an enhanced recovery rate. It is open a new way to use Al-ZnO nanocrystals as sensitive layer for gas sensor devices on flexible substrates.

Acknowledgment

The authors would like to acknowledge A. Combes for his technical support in this work.

References

[1] R. Kumar, O. Al-Dossary, G. Kumar, and A.Umar, "Zinc oxide nanostructures for NO_2 gas-sensor applications: A Review", Nano-Micro Letters, Vol. 7, Issue 2, pp 97-120, 2015, doi:10.1007/s40820-014-0023-3

[2] S.C Navale, et al., "EPR and DRS evidence for NO_2 sensing in Al-doped ZnO", Sensors and Actuators B Chemical 130(2): pp. 668-673, 2008, doi:10.1016/j.snb.2007.10.055

[3] J.D.Prades, et al.,"Equivalence between thermal and room temperature UV light-modulated responses of gas sensors based on individual SnO_2 Nanowires", Sensors and Actuators B: Chemical, Vol. 140, Issue 2, 2009, pp. 337-341, doi:10.1016/j.snb.2009.04.070

[4] M. Gaceur, et al. "Ligand-free synthesis of aluminium-doped zinc oxide nanocrystals and their use as optical spacers in color-tuned highly efficient organic solar cells", Adv. Funct. Mater. 26, pp. 243–253, 2016, doi:10.1002/adfm.201502929

Area and Speed Efficient Layout Design of Shift Registers using Nanometer Technology

Rajesh Mehra
ECE Department, NITTTR,
Chandigarh, U.T. India -160019
e-mail: rajeshmehra@yahoo.com

Priya Kaushal
ECE Department, NITTTR,
Chandigarh, U.T. India -160019
e-mail: pkaushal2407@gmail.com

Ayushi Gagneja
ECE Department, NITTTR,
Chandigarh, U.T. India -160019
e-mail:splendid.ayushi@gmail.com

***Abstract*— The paper presents an area and speed efficient CMOS layout design of shift register on 180 nanometer (nm) technology. The proposed shift register is designed using Serial In Serial Out (SISO) and Serial In Parallel Out (SIPO) techniques. Shift registers are commonly used in large number of sequential circuits and processors for temporary storage of data. The area and speed of developed layout designs are improved by optimized placement and routing for layout. The schematic and layout of both designs are simulated and analyzed using Cadence software. It can be observed from simulated results that the delay of SISO register is 0.97 ns and the delay of SIPO register is 0.71 ns. The SISO register shows 78.6% improvement in delay and SIPO register shows 27.46 % improvement in delay. The silicon area consumption of SISO register is 140.6 nm x 129.49 nm and SIPO register is 130.98 nm x 85.91 nm to provide cost effective solution for Very Large Scale Integration (VLSI) applications.**

Keywords- CMOS; Flip Flop; Shift Register; SISO; SIPO; VLSI.

I. Introduction

The new era of technology had a great impact on the field of VLSI, which is constantly under examination by many researchers throughout the world. It involves mainly increase in speed, reduction of area and power consumption [1]. Most vital component of the Integrated Circuits (ICs) for temporary storage of data is a Flip Flop. It stores a logical condition of one or more input signals using external clock [2]. Flip-flops are used in majority of computational circuits to store the data and provide adequate processing time to different circuits inside a system. In CMOS circuits, D Flip Flop (DFF) is essential building block and is responsible for the delay and total power dissipation calculations of any electronic system. Shift registers, which are created with the help of D flip-flops, have their intensive applications in various VLSI fields. The design of a shift register includes an N-bit shift register, made out of N number of Flip Flops [3][4][5].

A register is a circuit with two or more D Flip Flops connected together such that they all work exactly in the same way and a single clock synchronizes all the flip flops [6][7]. Each of these flip-flops has the ability of storing a single logic i.e., 0 or 1. There are limited compositions of 0 and 1 that can be stored into a register. These combinations are called the state of the register. Flip-Flops can store data in multiple sizes like 4, 8, 16, 32 or even 64 bits. Thus, several Flip Flops are combined to form a register to store whole data [8][9]. Fully custom 4-bit CMOS shift register consumes less power and less area as compare to semi custom and auto generated designs [10]. Double Edge Triggered Flip Flops are bi-stable flip-flop circuits in which data is latched at rising and falling edge of the clock signal. Using such flip-flops permits the rate of data processing to be preserved while using lower clock frequency. Therefore, power consumption in DETFF based circuits is less [11].

Three important factors related to nanometer technology based shift registers are power, delay and area. Most of the existing designs are concentrating on power factor without considering others. Some are working on power and area factors by ignoring delay factor which is very important these days for real time applications. So in order to fill these gaps related to shift register designs, optimized SISO and SIPO registers are developed in this paper to provide area efficient cost effective solution for real time applications. The rest of this paper is organized as follows. Section II presents shift register overview. In Section III, schematic design and simulations are presented. Section IV explains the layout design and analysis. Finally, Section V concludes the paper with the future work.

II. Shift Register

The main use of shift register is transmission of data after storage in serial or parallel manner. Serial means steady progression of bits in sequential manner and parallel means progression of all bits at the same time. Generally, shift registers are classified according to their structure into four different operating modes:

1. Serial-In Serial-Out (SISO) - The data is fed serially as input and the shifted output also occurs serially, one bit at a time in either left or right direction under clock control.

2. Serial-In Parallel-Out (SIPO) - The register is loaded with serial data, one bit at a time, with the output being stored in parallel form.

3. Parallel-In Serial-Out (PISO) - The data is loaded in parallel form into the register simultaneously and is shifted out of the register serially one bit at a time under clock control.

4. Parallel-In Parallel-Out (PIPO) - The parallel data is loaded simultaneously into the register, and transferred together to their respective outputs by the same clock pulse [12].

A. Serial In Serial Out Shift Register

Fig. 1 shows an example of four-bit SISO shift register using Single Bit Flip-Flop (SBFF).

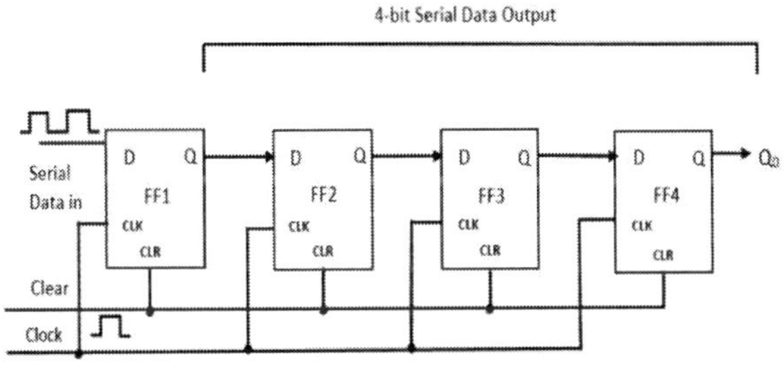

Figure 1. Serial-In Serial-Out Shift Register

A 4-bit SISO shift register is shown which takes four clock pulses to store the data bits and additional four cycles to transfer the data bits out from the register [12][13].

B. Serial-In to Parallel-Out (SIPO)

Fig. 2 shows a four-bit SIPO shift register which takes four clocks to process the input data and single clock to transfer the output data [10][11].

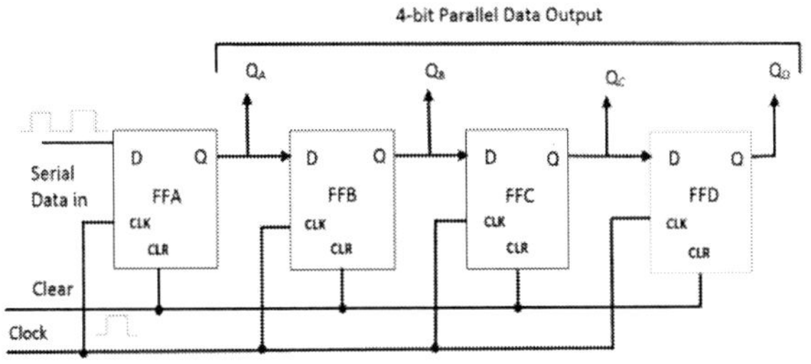

Figure 2. Serial-In to Parallel-Out 4-bit Shift Register

Every clock pulse impacts the register by shifting the data of every stage one place to the right. This data value at the output can now be read directly from QA. After the fourth clock pulse has ended the 4-bits of data are stored in the register and will remain there provided clocking of the register has stopped.

III. Schematic Design Simulation

The schematic of SISO register has been designed and simulated using 1.8V operating voltage on 180nm technology. Fig. 3 shows the schematic design of D flip-flop using NAND modules with power consumption of 746.8mW and delay of 0.245ns.

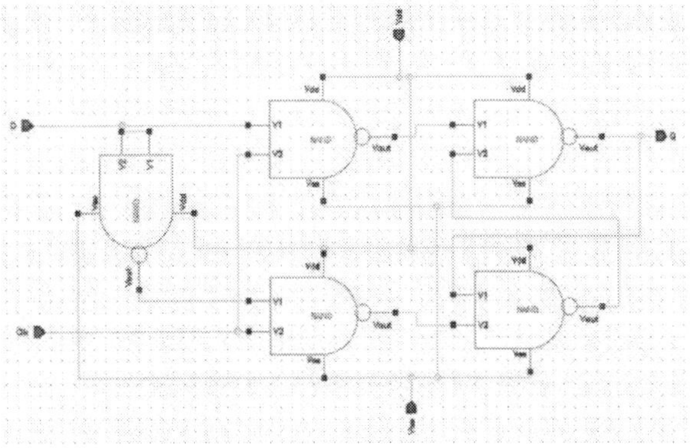

Figure 3. Schematic Design of D Flip-Flop

D-Flip Flop module was created and four such modules were combined together to design SISO register schematic as shown in Fig. 4. The developed SISO register has shown power consumption of 0.549mW and delay of 0.97ns.

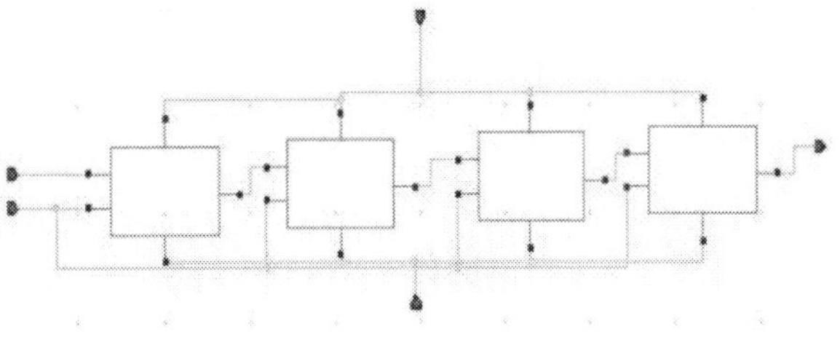

Figure 4. Schematic of SISO Shift Register

Analog simulation of designed SISO register has been performed for logic verification. The transient and DC responses of proposed SISO register are shown in Fig. 5 and Fig. 6 respectively.

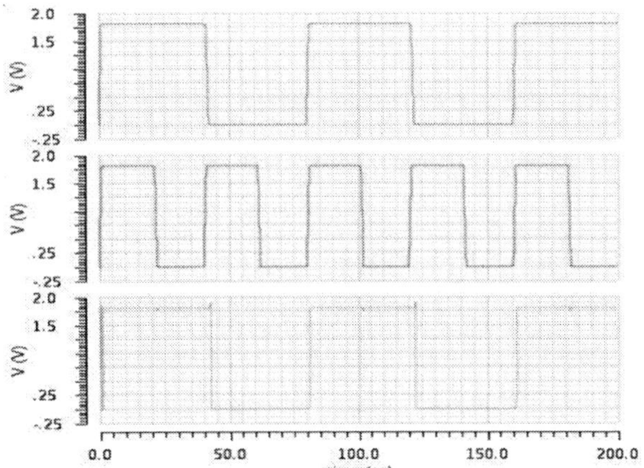

Figure 5. Transient Response of SISO Shift Register

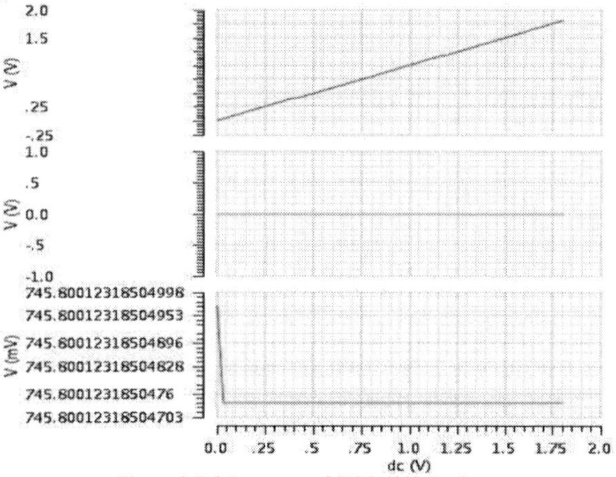

Figure 6. DC Response of SISO Shift Register

To improve the speed factor SIPO shift register schematic is designed as shown in Fig. 7. The developed SIPO register has shown power consumption of 0.5493 and delay of 0.71ns.

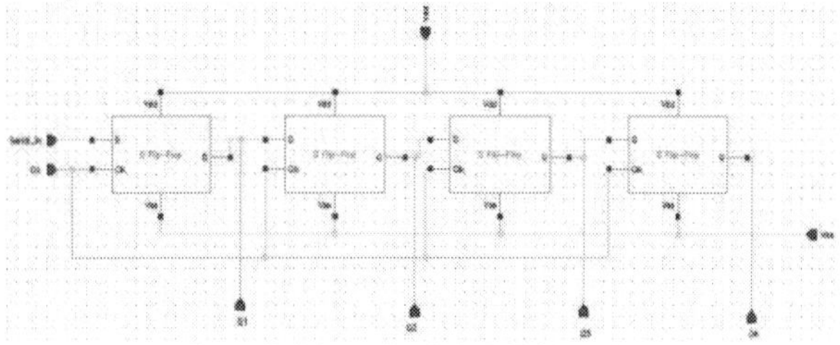
Figure 7. Schematic of SIPO Shift Register

The logic of developed SIPO register has been verified using analog simulation. The transient and DC responses of proposed SIPO register are shown in Fig. 8 and Fig. 9 respectively.

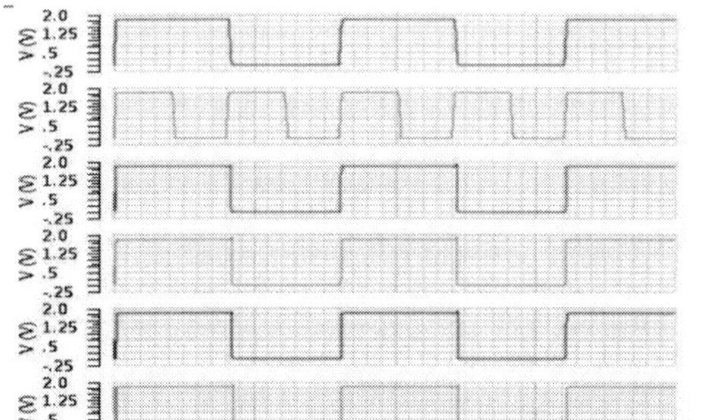

Figure 8. Transient Response of SIPO Shift Register

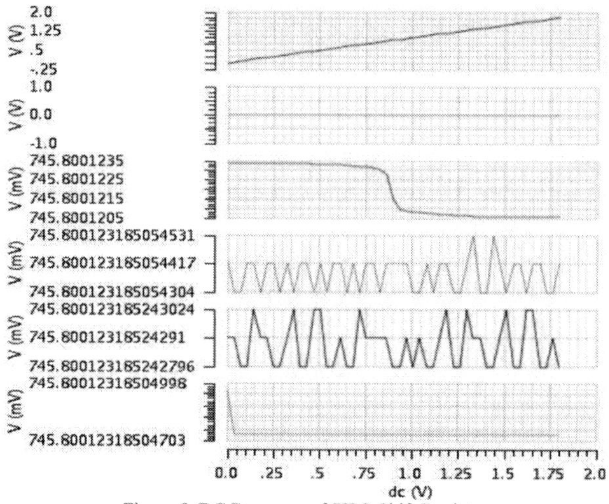

Figure 9. DC Response of SIPO Shift Register

After the evaluation of circuits is done with the help of simulations, then we proceed to the final step i.e., layout of shift registers.

IV. Layout Design Analysis

D-Flip Flop layout is developed using optimized NAND gates which consumes an area of 36.945mm x 33.44mm as shown in Fig. 10.

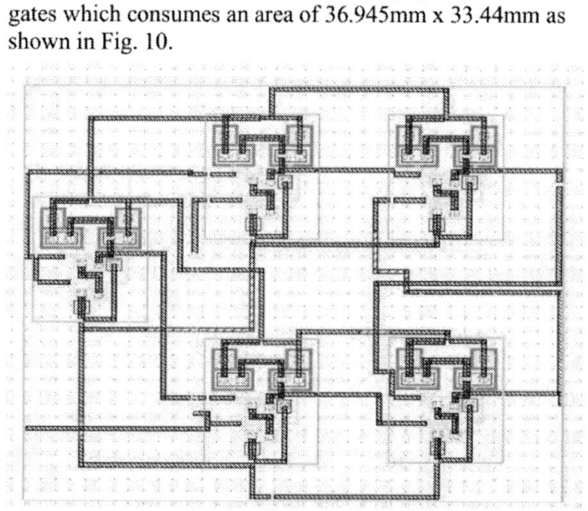
Figure 10. Layout Design of D flip-flop

D-Flip Flop layout module is created and four such modules are combined together to develop final layout of SISO register as shown in Fig. 11. The proposed SISO register layout has shown area consumption of 130.98nm x 85.91nm and power consumption of 0.536mW. Finally layout Vs schematic (LVS) comparison has been performed to verify the design performance as shown in Fig. 12.

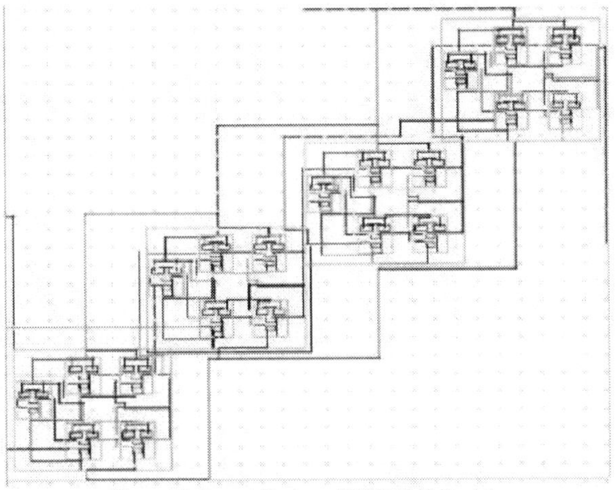

Figure 11. Layout Design of SISO Shift Register

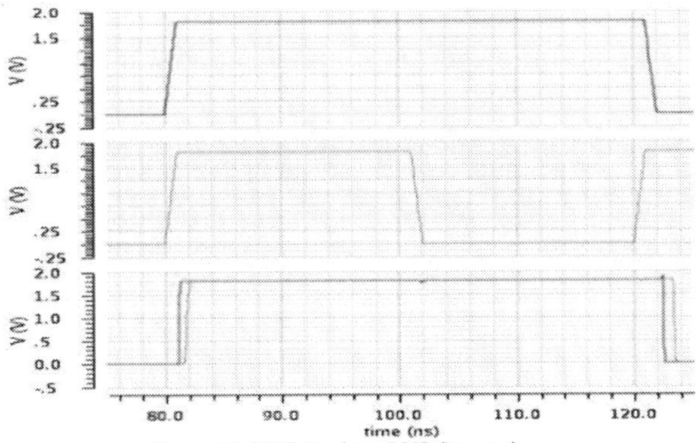

Figure 12. SISO Register LVS Comparison

Similarly layout of SIPO register has been developed with D-Flip Flop by using optimized placement and routing as shown in Fig. 13. The proposed SIPO register layout has shown area consumption of 130.98nm x 85.91nm and power consumption of 0.43mW.

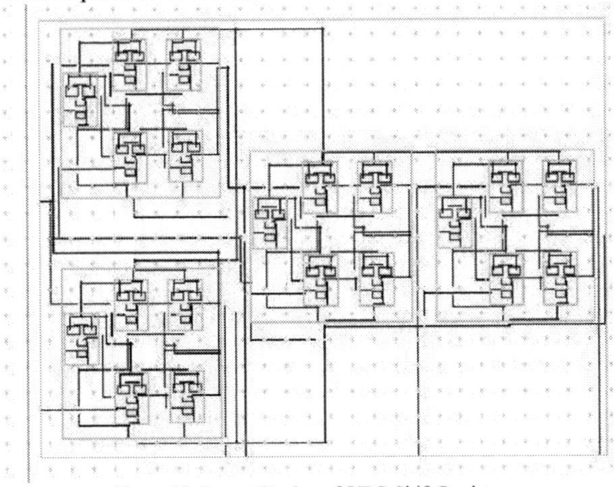

Figure 13. Layout Design of SIPO Shift Register

Layout Vs Schematic (LVS) comparison of SIPO shift register has been performed to verify the performance of developed design as shown in Fig. 14.

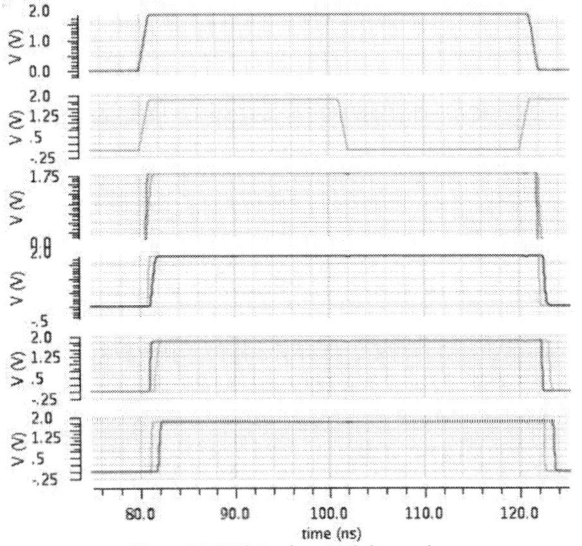

Figure 14. SIPO Register LVS Comparison

Table 1 shows the area and speed analysis of proposed SISO and SIPO registers. It can be observed from the table that SIPO design provides better speed as compared to SISO design, while consuming same amount of area.

TABLE I. PERFORMANCE ANALYSIS OF PROPOSED DESIGNS

Design Technique	Area (nm^2)	Delay(ns)
SISO	140.6*129.49	0.97
SIPO	130.98*85.91	0.71

TABLE II. DELAY COMPARISON

Design Technique	Existing Design [13]	Proposed Design
SISO	1.71 ns	0.97 ns
SIPO	0.905 ns	0.71 ns

The delay comparison of proposed designs with existing designs [13] is shown in Table 2. It shows that proposed SISO register provides 78.6% improvement in delay and SIPO register provides 27.46% improvement in delay as compared to existing designs.

V. Conclusion and Future Work

Area and speed efficient 4-bit SISO shift register and 4-bit SIPO shift register are designed on 180 nm technology. These designs were improved using optimized placement and routing technique. The proposed designs were developed by using D Flip Flop modules based on optimized NAND gate layout. The developed SIPO register has shown better speed as compared to SISO register by consuming same area. The proposed SISO register has shown 78.6% improvement in delay and proposed SIPO design has shown 27.46% improvement in delay as compared to existing designs. The proposed optimized designs have consumed very less silicon area to provide cost effective solution for VLSI applications. In future work, designs can be further optimized by developing improved placement and routing algorithm.

References

[1] B. Nikoli´c, "Design in the Power-Limited Scaling Regime," IEEE Transactions on Electron Devices, Vol. 55, pp. 71-83, January 2008.

[2] S. Sharma and B. Kaushal, "Shift Register Design Using Two Bit Flip-Flop," IEEE Conference on Recent Advances in Engineering and Computational Sciences (RAECS), pp. 463-468, 2014.

[3] M. Arunlakshman, T. Dineshkumar, and N. Mathan, "Performance Evaluation of 6 Transistor D-Flip Flop based Shift Registers using GDI Technique," International Journal of Advanced Research in Computer and Communication Engineering (IJARCCE), Vol. 3, Issue 3, pp. 5858-5861, March 2014.

[4] N. Rapartiwar and V. Kapse, "Design of Serial in Serial out And Serial In Parallel out Shift Register Using Double Edge Triggered D Flip Flop," International Journal of Emerging Technology and Advanced Engineering (IJETAE), Vol. 4, Issue 7, pp. 505-508, July 2014.

[5] B. D. Yang, "Low-Power and Area-Efficient Shift Register Using Pulsed Latches," IEEE Transactions On Circuits And Systems, Vol. 62, No. 6, pp. 1564-1571, June 2015.

[6] D. J. Reddy and A. V. Paramkusam, "A Novel Approach to Power Optimized Memory Organization By Using Multi-Bit Flip-Flops," International Journal of Emerging Trends in Electrical and Electronics (IJETEE), Vol. 10, Issue. 9, October 2014.

[7] P. K. Chakravarti and R. Mehra, "Layout design of D Flip Flop for Power and Area Reduction," International Journal of Scientific Research Engineering & Technology (IJSRET), pp. 154-158, 14-15 March, 2015.

[8] F. Ahmad, M. Mustafa, N. A. Wani, and F. A. Mir, "A novel idea of pseudo-code generator in quantum-dot cellular automata (QCA)," International Journal for Simulation and Multidisciplinary Design Optimization (IJSMDO), pp. 1-8, 2014.

[9] M. A. S. Bhuiyan, H. N. B. Rosly, M. B. I. Reaz, K. N. Minhad, and H. Husain, "Advances on CMOS Shift Registers for Digital Data Storage," TELKOMNIKA Indonesian Journal of Electrical Engineering, Vol. 12, pp. 3849-3862, May 2014.

[10] P. Srivastava and R. Mehra, "Design Analysis Of Area Efficient 4 Bit Shift Register Using Cmos Technology," International Journal of Electrical and Electronics Engineering (IJEEE), Vol. 7, Issue 01, January 2015.

[11] D. I. Praveen, T. Ravi, and E. Logashanmugam, "Design and Analysis of High Performance Double Edge Triggered D-Flip Flop based Shift Registers," International Journal of Emerging Technology and Advanced Engineering (IJETAE), Vol. 3, Issue 2, pp. 274-278, February 2013

[12] M. K. Singh and Rajeev Kumar, "Simulation of Enhanced Pulse Triggered Flip Flop with High Performance Applications," International Journal of Engineering Sciences & Research Technology (IJESRT), pp. 489-493, January 2015.

[13] L. S. Kiran and M Valarmathi, "Design of Shift Registers using SEU-tolerant Isolated-DICE latch," International Journal of Engineering Research & Technology (IJERT), Vol. 4, Issue 04, pp. 620-624, April 2015.